Teach Your Baby to Sign

Teach Your Baby to Sign

AN ILLUSTRATED GUIDE TO SIMPLE SIGN LANGUAGE FOR BABIES

Monica Beyer

FAIR WINDS
PRESS
BEVERLY, MASSACHUSETTS

First published in the USA in 2007 by
Fair Winds Press, a member of
Quayside Publishing Group
100 Cummings Center
Suite 406-L
Beverly, MA 01915-6101
www.fairwindspress.com

11 10 09   3 4 5

ISBN-13: 978-1-59233-273-1

ISBN-10: 1-59233-273-0

Library of Congress Cataloging-in-Publication Data

Beyer, Monica, 1974-
Teach your baby to sign : an illustrated guide to simple sign language for babies / Monica Beyer.
p. cm.
ISBN-10: 1-59233-273-0
ISBN-13: 978-1-59233-273-1
1. Nonverbal communication in infants. 2. Interpersonal communication in infants.
3. Sign language. 4. Infants--Language. 5. American Sign Language. I. Title.
BF720.C65B494 2007
419'.1--dc22

2007016558

Cover design by Mary Ann Smith
Book design by Laura H. Couallier, Laura Herrmann Design
Illustrations by William Michael Wanke
Photography by:
Allan Penn Photography (pages: cover, 9, 25, 163)
David Stotzer, Cape Ann Photography (pages: 28, 47, 95, 102, 103)
Glenn Scott Photography (pages: 51, 59, 71, 115, 120, 155, 161)
Michelle Wettengel (pages: 23, 37, 55, 75, 78, 79, 108, 125, 128, 141, 148, 149)

Printed and bound in China

Dedication

This book is dedicated to my
Nan—for the joy and inspiration she
has given to me and everyone who
has had the pleasure of knowing her.
I love you Nan.

Table of Contents

• • •

Introduction

Teach Your Baby to Sign!

Why Sign?

Welcome to the wonderful world of signing with babies. I am sharing this world with you, from one parent to another, because of the fun that I have had as a signing mom. I signed with two of my children (Corbin and Lauren) but not with the first—simply because I didn't know about signing when Dagan was small (oh, but how I wish I had).

In 2000, when Corbin was eleven months old, I was watching a news program that featured a baby girl who used sign language to show her mom that she was in pain because of teething and wanted medicine. I was intrigued and quickly went to the Internet to see what I could find out.

I bought a book online about baby sign language and was very excited to give it a try. Corbin, after about four weeks of my signing "milk" to him when he nursed, began signing back to me. I was over the moon. We continued our signing, adding more vocabulary, and he became a proficient signer.

I was so inspired by my success with my own baby that I wanted to share what I had learned with other parents, and so I created my own Web site, www.signingbaby.com, in 2000.

Signing is one of the most interesting, fun, exciting, and *useful* things you can do as a parent. It provides you with amazing insight into your baby's world. When I was changing Lauren's diaper one day, for example, she began signing "dog" instead of signing "change" as she often did. I wasn't sure what she was trying to communicate at first, but her gesture became more pronounced and she indicated, by pointing, the other side of the room. I looked over and realized that she wanted to hold her stuffed dog. If she hadn't known the sign for "dog" I never would have realized exactly what she was talking about!

Sign language, in addition, encourages the following:

- Early Communication
- Vocabulary
- Speech
- Trust
- Interaction

Signing has many benefits. For instance, your child will not only be able to tell you when he is hungry, cold, or suffering from an earache, but when he sees a bird in a tree or needs help getting his favorite toy from a shelf. Signing helped my children feel that they could come to me with their ideas, needs, and wants, and they knew that I would more than likely be able to understand and help them—all without saying a word.

One day, Corbin was playing with a variety of toys on the floor and he came across a container that held his favorite blocks. He was unable to pry the lid off, but instead of fussing or crying he turned to me and signed "help." Signing not only helped him accomplish a physical task—with assistance from mom—it allowed him to continue playing without interruption or, more importantly, without getting upset and possibly spiraling into a meltdown from frustration.

The gift of signing helps your baby communicate well before she has the verbal ability to do so. This can make a year's worth of difference, or maybe even more— a wonderful head start in understanding your baby's wants, needs, and interests.

Signing can be helpful well into the toddler years. When children begin speaking, they typically learn a few words at a time, experiencing significant gaps between what they can say and what they would like to say. Signing readily fills these gaps; watch a child simultaneously "sign and speak" a sentence and you'll see how. Communicating in sign language can help toddlers overcome a lot of the frustration that can accompany a need to communicate without the physical ability to do so yet.

This book will not only show you the steps needed to make signing successful in your home, but it also features 200 signs as well as helpful tips for teaching them and incorporating them into your daily life.

Using American Sign Language

This book teaches 200 signs that are from an actual signed language—American Sign Language, otherwise known as ASL.

Why I Chose ASL

I have chosen to use—and teach you—ASL signs for many reasons. One is that it encourages communication with deaf people—an entire segment of society that we weren't able to communicate with at all at one time. Two, it's beneficial within your own family. If you have a baby and one or more older children, the older kids will see you signing and learn too, which can help them communicate with a younger sibling.

Signing also helps children learn that there is more to communication than just speech. It teaches them that hand gestures, body movements, and facial expressions can also serve as communication tools, even when not accompanied by spoken words. Knowing this, children and adults may have more success understanding those who don't speak the same language and may be able to communicate more effectively in general as they get older. Teaching children sign language allows them to be comfortable using physical gestures from an early age.

There are many materials out in the marketplace that can help you learn signs to teach to your baby. Most of these products are ASL-based, mainly for consistency reasons. You wouldn't want to show your child a DVD with signs that are not the same as the ones you have learned from a book or online! How confusing would that be?

You might run into a problem where your DVD shows you one sign and this book (or another book) shows you a different one. This is because signs vary from place to place, even within the same country, much like a spoken language. For example, you could order a sub, a hoagie, or a grinder, and still get the same thing. In this case, choose a specific sign that your baby will see most often, so if a particular signing DVD is her absolute favorite, you might use the signs in it if they differ in any way from another reference you are using.

A Brief History of Baby Signing

The baby signing movement officially began in the early 1980s with the ground-breaking research of Dr. Linda Acredolo and Dr. Susan Goodwyn. They began conducting academic research on the subject and eventually published the first baby signing book in 1996, which led to a movement that has gained momentum ever since. Their first book focused on creating your own "baby" signs, but the second edition incorporated more ASL than its predecessor.

In the 1970s, another pioneer, Dr. Joseph Garcia, began noticing communication and interaction between deaf parents and their hearing babies and the ease with which the babies picked up sign language from their parents. A decade later, he began doing his own research with hearing babies of hearing parents and was inspired and astounded by what he witnessed. His first book, *Toddler Talk: The First Signs of Intelligent Life*, was published in 1994. A subsequent book, *Sign with your Baby*, came out in 1999; this was actually the book from which I learned how to sign with my first signing baby.

As I mentioned before, I first heard about signing with babies in 2000, and even then it wasn't a widely known activity. I received a lot of strange looks and even criticism from many people, but persevered. Even though I had no personal experience with baby signing, I thought the idea made a lot of sense and believed that it would happen. Once Corbin started signing back and I realized how sign language allowed him to communicate specific ideas with me, I was hooked. Corbin amazed everyone by his signing abilities as he learned more vocabulary signs. By the time Lauren was born in 2002, signing for babies had become more popular, in part because many childcare providers were beginning to incorporate signing into their daily routines.

Then, in 2004, thanks to the movie "Meet the Fockers," which featured a darling signing baby, signing exploded in popularity and more and more parents wanted to learn how to sign with their babies.

Now when someone finds out that I am involved in signing with babies, they almost always have heard of it in some context before. Their granddaughter may have learned it at daycare, they may have seen the movie, or they may be signing to their baby themselves.

Myth Busting

There are several myths that you might have heard about signing with babies. This chapter will help you understand why they are not true.

Signing Does Not Delay Speech

The biggest concern that many parents have when they first hear about signing with babies is that somehow, in some way, it delays a child's natural ability to acquire spoken language. I am happy to report that this is not true.

The easiest way to illustrate why this is not true is to share a simple analogy. In normal human development, babies go through a series of phases, or milestones, that parents can look for and note in their baby books. One of the areas of development that causes a lot of excitement for parents is mobility—the art of getting around. Generally, babies roll over, first one way then the next, then try a variety of scooting mechanisms, followed by crawling, pulling themselves up, walking while holding on to furniture, and, finally, walking alone.

Have you ever heard parents fret about their child's crawling holding them back from walking, providing them with a crutch and making them lazy? Probably not. But

I've heard many people worry that if babies know how to sign, they will merely continue to sign in bliss, never having the need or desire to learn to express themselves verbally.

If you think of signing as a bridge to verbal communication, as it rightly is, you will have an easier time understanding how signing does not *delay* speech but rather *enhances* it.

Crawling (or scooting or rolling) enables babies to get around, and it encourages their natural drive to accomplish independent walking. Saying it is an impediment to learning to walk would sound ridiculous. Signing, in the same way, allows small children to have their needs and desires understood well before they would be able to speak, and their desire to communicate only increases as a result.

Several academic studies also did not find that signing delays speech. Dr. Linda Acredolo and Dr. Susan Goodwyn, authors of *Baby Signs*, began researching teaching sign language to pre-verbal babies more than twenty years ago. They discovered that not only did sign language not delay the babies' speech, it enhanced it. In addition, at the age of eight, the signing babies scored higher on IQ tests than their non-signing peers.

Also, Dr. Michelle Anthony and Dr. Reyna Lindert, authors of *Signing Smart with Babies and Toddlers*, discovered similar findings when they studied children who had been signed to using the "Signing Smart" method in 2005.

There has been research conducted that also shows that signing helps children with developmental delays and disorders. In 1993, Marita Hopman, Ph.D., wrote in the magazine *Down Syndrome Today* that teaching sign language to a baby with Down syndrome is extremely helpful. Sign language is also recommended for a variety of other children, including those with apraxia of speech and autism.

Signing is Easy

I have also heard that using ASL is far too complicated for the parent—perhaps the naysayer envisions long nights of ASL classroom instruction? How would you, or anyone, have time for that? Fortunately this is simply not the case.

I'm happy to report that I didn't know a lick of ASL besides the alphabet when I started on my signing quest with Corbin in 2000, and both he and his baby sister wound up knowing more than 100 signs before they gave them up. Parents generally learn right along with their children, sign by sign. No mandatory classes, no late night studying, no quizzes are necessary—just access to educational information when your child needs a new sign and you are good to go.

What I did, and what I recommend you do, too, is learn a handful of signs at a time, at the same time as your baby or toddler. Incorporating the signs into my life took a little getting used to but once they were in, they were in! It became second nature to sign.

By breaking the process down into bite-sized chunks, I was able to learn plenty of signs and never feel overwhelmed.

For someone who went into this process knowing little to no sign language to have as much roaring success as I did with my signing babies has to be a testament to the ease of signing with babies. I started out not knowing any actual signs and learned right along with my second baby, who wound up able to sign more than 100 words. Then, when my third child was a baby, I was able to teach her additional signs. She had a vocabulary of more than 200 signs by the time she gave them up. And now, just a few years later, I am authoring a sign language book.

ASL is the Right Sign Language

I have also heard that using ASL (or any other form of official signed language) is too difficult for the baby to learn and reproduce as some of the signs are pretty precise and involve particular finger motions or positions.

Some say that ASL signs are too difficult for small hands, which haven't learned fine motor skills yet, to make. This actually starts to make some sense until you think about how small children learn spoken language. Parents are NOT advised to speak "down" to their children simply because they are not developmentally capable of saying the word. You talk with them about their milk and their blanket, yet they may make sounds such as "ma" and "ba." You are fully aware that, over time, they will refine their speech as their muscles grow more mature and they will say the word correctly.

The exact same thing applies to sign language. Babies will attempt any sign that you do if they are interested in communicating it with you. It may not be 100 percent correct or precise at first, but they will modify it as they grow and mature. You will learn what their approximations are, and as long as you continue to demonstrate the ASL version they will eventually get it.

So there really is no need to simplify the signs that you show your baby. Your baby will approximate signs just as she will words when she's learning to speak, and over time, as your baby grows and her fine motor development matures, she will refine her signs until they are correct.

How to Sign

As mentioned before, signing with babies is easy and not difficult at all. However, there is a simple method to use and tips to help you get the most success from your efforts.

Starting Out

You can start signing with your baby at any time. Seriously! It really isn't too early or too late—ever—with a child.

However, the optimal time that I generally recommend is anywhere from six to eight months old. Babies have often mastered the art of sitting up on their own by this age and often (as you will see later) when they are busy trying to master a physical developmental task they will focus strongly on it and not show interest in signs.

However, there is no harm is starting earlier, as deaf parents around the world will tell you. This doesn't guarantee that they will sign to you earlier. It might actually cause more frustration because it takes that much longer for the baby to "get it," but it can help you become accustomed to the act of signing and you will find yourself growing more comfortable signing naturally.

On the other hand, what if you don't find out about signing until your baby is a year old, or even older? It's still not too late to start, especially if your baby doesn't have a large spoken vocabulary. I didn't know about signing with babies until Corbin was eleven months old and he still benefited greatly from the experience. When Lauren was an infant and I started signing with her, the boys (then four and seven) really enjoyed learning (and in Corbin's case, re-learning) the signs.

How many signs should you start with?

This depends, ultimately, on you. I would recommend starting out with six to twelve signs, but you may be comfortable starting out with only one. It's best to start out with several signs each of two distinct varieties: those that your baby will experience on a daily or routine basis, and those that your baby might find quite exciting and motivating. This way you give your baby ample opportunity and exposure when you concentrate on these signs.

For example, many parents begin with the sign for "milk." This is often one of baby's most common activities and is a very popular choice for the diaper set. Depending on your child's age and eating routines, you could add the signs for "eat" and "water," or maybe "sleep" and "bath." These are signs that your child can learn any day, every day, and that you will be able to do over and over.

To choose a motivating sign, pay careful attention to what your child shows a great deal of interest in. Perhaps she is excited by her stuffed animals—the tiger in particular. Maybe she is enamored of her small collection of hats. If you find that she has a favorite object or activity, learn the sign for it.

It's also fine to just choose a single sign and start with that, adding more to your vocabulary depending on what she shows an interest in.

How do you teach signing, anyway?

Fortunately teaching babies to sign is not like teaching multiplication tables. You don't have to drill it into them with flash cards or sit in front of them, repeating a sign over and over.

Once you have chosen a group of signs to begin with, all you have to do is sign each one when either the activity is happening or your baby catches sight of something. Sounds simple, doesn't it? Well, it is, and as long as you keep a few things in mind it will be easy.

- Be sure to consistently sign the same sign the same way every time you sign it.
- For activities, you can sign them either directly before you do something (e.g., "We're going to 'change' your diaper now.") or while it's going on (e.g., "Are you drinking your 'milk'?").
- For interesting sights or sounds, you may have to sign in a baby's line of sight for him to notice you.
- You can also sign *on* a baby's body. Lauren was enthralled by our dog Choopie and wouldn't tear her eyes away from her for anything, so I would reach down and pat her thigh. This caused her to not only notice me but it helped her make the physical connection to the sign.
- Be sure to speak as you sign. Think of signing as punctuation for your sentence, emphasizing the important vocabulary that you wish your child to pick up on.

As a reference, we have included the signs for each letter of the alphabet in Chapter 9: "Signing the Alphabet." Some signs incorporate the use of letters. For example, "zoo" is signed by spelling out the letters "z-o-o." For "lizard," you would make the sign for "L" and move it up toward your elbow as your finger bends and wiggles.

How long will it be before my baby starts signing?

It really varies from one child to the next, just as everything else does. I started signing with Corbin at eleven months and Lauren at six months, and they both took about four weeks to sign back to me. It can take as little as a week for an older child to months for a younger one (generally, although not in all cases, the older a child is the quicker she will be to sign back to you).

How will you know if a baby wants to learn a new sign?

At first, signing will be new to you and your baby, and it will be extremely exciting once he learns his first few signs. Once he realizes how wonderful signing is and how it can not only get his needs met but also his wants attended to he may request new signs from you.

It may not seem apparent at first to you but my children would point to an object and they would get that "look" in their eyes, which meant, "What's the sign for this, Mom?" If we were planning an outing I would look up a few new themed signs in advance, which is why I wanted to categorize this book by subject matter. So if you're going to the zoo, be sure to stock up on animal signs!

What does "approximation" mean?

In much the same way that a baby will do her best to say a word but it comes out as a simplified version (or even completely different), the same thing happens sometimes when a baby is trying to do a sign that is a little more complicated. The baby is approximating one gesture as best as she can but the meaning is still the same.

She will sometimes make vague movements with her hands (similar to ones that are less precise than the real version) or make wild multiple looping versions of the real thing. You might also notice her substituting different ones for signs that require touching a body part, like when Lauren signed "dog" she patted her chest instead of her thigh.

It's a good idea to keep all of this in mind as your baby starts signing because it's a possibility that your baby may be making more signs than you are aware of!

Troubleshooting

While signing is easy and soon becomes intuitive, there are a few common obstacles that often come up. If you know about them in advance it's a huge benefit to you because then you don't feel like you're either doing it wrong or that there is something wrong with your baby!

Common Obstacles and Possible Solutions

If your baby...	Then you should...
... signs the same thing for everything. Example: Signs "milk" for cereal, cracker, more food, etc.	... continue to sign correctly and consistently. Solution: If you know baby wants "more" and not "milk," be sure to sign "more" while clearly saying it.
... makes the same gesture but you think he means different things. Example: The hand shape for "ball," "hurt," and "shoes" are all signs that bring both hands together at the midpoint of the body and can look very similar when coming from a baby's hands. ... make sure that you pay close attention to the context in which your baby is signing.	... make sure that you pay close attention to the context in which your baby is signing. Note: Watch out for these and other approximations—this type of confusion is quite common!
... stops signing. Example: Your baby has successfully signed to you for a month or two and suddenly begins trying to crawl and abandons all of her signs. ... keep on signing!	... keep on signing! Note: Often when a baby concentrates hard on achieving a physical development mile-stone she might devote all of her attention to that task and resume the signing when she accomplishes it.
... takes "forever" to sign back. Example: Often parents write me and ask, "I don't think my child is able to sign. Will he ever sign?"	... look for signs that you might have missed and don't give up. Solution: Some babies just take longer to "get it." There is no real magical timetable that babies follow, just like any other area of development. As long as your baby is pre-verbal, I wouldn't stop signing. Try to create more signing situations using some of the activities in this book and hopefully your efforts will soon pay off!

Milestones

Just like speech development, babies tend to follow a particular path as they learn to sign with you.

Receptive Learning

Receptive language refers to words whose meanings you understand when you hear them. The same holds true for signing—often a baby will understand the meaning of a sign well before he is able to successfully use it himself. For example, if you verbally ask your baby if she'd like some milk, and your baby acts excited, she understands the word you've said and thus has gained the receptive language vocabulary for "milk." Receptive language, then, is also enhanced when your baby understands a sign. Receptive language can give you a clue that your baby may be nearing the time of making his first sign.

Here's what to look for:

- Obvious reaction when you sign
- Eyes light up
- Baby wiggles in glee
- Arms flap

I definitely had the best reactions when I signed "milk." They knew it was milky time!

Expressive Language

Expressive language is what your baby can actually say or sign. This starts out as your baby's first sign, which is definitely one you want to add to the baby book!

Here's what to look for:

- Seemingly random motions that are the same every day
- Waving at nursing/bottle time
- Excitement when baby moves her hands
- (Sometimes) grunting or other vocalization

Using One Sign for Everything

This happened with both of my signing babies in the beginning. Once they learned "milk," everything was "milk." Their cereal, the outdoors, daddy, crackers…I could go on and on! Basically everything that they wanted became the sign that they knew.

This is extremely common and is actually a good sign to look for. This means that the baby has internalized signing and knows that to request something, he or she needs to sign for it.

Here's what to look for:

- The first sign to be accomplished and established
- Signing something when you know he doesn't mean it

This stage does take a little patience, but all you need to do is start demonstrating signs for items that he's showing a lot of interest in. This is a great way to pick new signs to learn!

Signs Looking the Same

This was addressed in the Troubleshooting section, but generally once a baby begins signing on a more regular basis and has learned more than one sign, often some of the signs look the same.

This is very common and can be compared to a baby learning to talk. Good examples are the words baby, bear, bottle, and balloon. These all may start out as a single or double consonant-vowel combination—in other words, "ba ba." In much the same way, signs with a similar hand shape may start out as the same vague gesture, but over time he will refine his signs.

Here's what to look for:

- A good example is everything looking like the "more" sign
- A frustrated baby if you don't understand the right way

What you can do to help is to use context to decipher his signs and always reinforce with the correct version.

The Signing Explosion

This stage is a lot of fun. We've been through it twice and enjoyed it both times. This stage is also the point where you can really learn a lot about what your baby is interested in. Lauren's great interest from an early age was animals, and she loved to point to as many as she could so she could learn the signs for them all.

Once your baby has learned many signs and she knows that signing will help get her what she wants and needs, in addition to helping her talk about what she sees and experiences, something suddenly seems to click and she'll want to know the signs for *everything*.

You may feel overwhelmed as your baby's signing teacher. You will want to have this book very close by as your baby goes around the house, pointing to various favorite objects and looking at you with eyes that seem to ask: "What's the sign for this?"

Here's what to look for:

- Baby requesting signs with pointing or other body language
- Baby begins learning and repeating signs back to you at a rapid pace
- Baby seems like a beautiful little signing sponge and cannot get enough!

This stage is a jumping-off point to the rest of your baby's signing experiences. Once she knows she can get a new sign from you she will probably continue to request signs, and the best thing you can do is keep learning the signs right along with her.

Chapter
1

Routines and Needs

Using Common Activities

The signs in this chapter are ones for activities or things that your baby will encounter as she goes about her daily business. Generally, every day your baby will get a diaper change, take a bath, go somewhere, see you cleaning, take a nap, and eventually she will learn to brush her teeth and wash her hands.

Since she does these things so often, you should find it easy to work these signs into her daily routine. I would consider these to be naturally occurring opportunities and as you grow more confident signing and work them into your day, your baby will see these as a part of everyday life and will incorporate them into her first vocabulary—her signing vocabulary!

Picking out a few of your child's most common activities (for example, "bed" and "bath") would be a great way to start using the signs from this chapter. Gradually work up your vocabulary to include as many as you feel comfortable doing—or, as in our case, as many as your child indicates that she would like to learn (my daughter Lauren, once she started signing, ate up signs faster than her goldfish crackers).

Look for other opportunities that may not be totally obvious. Signs like "open" and "up" have lots of different applications and can be used in more than one situation. Important signs like "all done" and "help" have the same characteristic and may prove to be your and your baby's favorite signs because they can help eliminate stress, frustration, and tears.

Again

Again

Tap the palm of one hand with the fingertips of your other, bent, hand.

"Simon's ability to sign 'all done' stopped him from whining until I guessed what he wanted!"

—Robin, mother of two-year-old Simon

All Done

This sign starts with both palms facing up. Flip them over and out, as if you were brushing crumbs from your shirt after a satisfying meal.

All Done

Quick Tip

This may become one of your child's favorite signs. It has so many uses—from indicating that she is done eating, to being finished playing peek-a-boo, and everything in between!

"I am a daycare teacher, and I wanted to incorporate signing into our daily activities. We started with the sign for 'all done' after every meal and snack. I would say, 'All done!' in a cheery voice and do the sign. After a week or so most of my infants had picked it up."

—Lauren, child care provider

Bath

With both fists, make circular rubbing motions on your torso, as if you are washing yourself.

Quick Tip

Sign "bath" before you put your baby in the tub as well as during her bath. Talk about what she will experience in the bath and the sign should help her make an association with the activity itself.

Bath

Blanket

Start your hands near your belly and pull them up to your chest. Picture yourself lying in bed and pulling up your blanket and you've got it!

Quick Tip

This sign is good for pairing with "bed." As your baby grows older she may even match the two signs up herself. It can also easily be used alone, particularly if your child is like mine and loves to take her favorite blanket around the house with her.

Blanket

Bed

Bed

Put both hands together, tilt to the side, and rest your head on your hands.

Quick Tip

This is another daily routine sign that you can use before or during the activity. Asking, "Are you ready for bed?" while signing "bed" will help your baby connect the meaning and the sign. And signing "bed" as you either talk about her bed or as you are placing her in it will do the same.

Broken

Hold both fists together and quickly pull them apart, as if you were snapping something in half.

Broken

Quick Tip

Unfortunately your baby may come across a broken toy or something that you've accidentally broken (such as a glass). This is a good sign for illustrating the breakage itself or warning her away from a broken item.

Brush Teeth

Brush Teeth

Bare your teeth and "brush" them with your index finger.

Quick Tip

This is an excellent sign that should get a lot of use. Once you start brushing his teeth, show him this sign. My daughter really resisted teeth brushing at the beginning and our signing "brush teeth" before we even started helped her transition to the activity.

Change

Put both fists together, one on top of the other, and then quickly change their position so that the fist that was on the bottom is now on the top.

Change

Quick Tip

This sign is useful for signing about diaper changing. Our hope was that our children would learn to show us that they needed a change once they got the sign down, and it definitely worked. You can consider it a precursor for toilet learning as well by giving them the vocabulary early on for their potty needs.

Clean

Wipe one hand with the other, as though you were washing dishes.

Clean

Quick Tip

There are many uses for the "clean" sign. You can sign it, for example, when you are doing the dishes or picking up the playroom. If you're going about, doing household chores, and you notice that your baby is interested in what you are doing, be sure to talk to him about your activities and sign to him.

Clothes

This sign is done by running your hands down your chest a few times. Think of clothes hanging from your body and it should help you remember this sign!

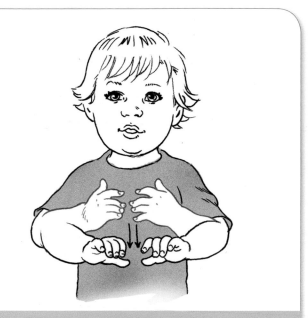

Clothes

Quick Tip

This sign might also remind you of brushing out wrinkles in clothes. Sign it while dressing your baby or when you go shopping for a new outfit for her.

Coat

Take both "Y" hands and move them from your shoulders to your chest. This should remind you of putting a coat on. See Chapter 9 for how to sign the letter "Y."

Quick Tip

Sign "coat" before you put your baby's coat on while going out on a cold day. The motion may take her a while to understand but because it looks like what it stands for it might be an easy one to catch on to, particularly if she sees you doing it a lot!

Coat

Cold

Put both fists up at chest level and shake back and forth a little bit. Picture yourself feeling cold and shivering!

Cold

Quick Tip

This sign has many uses. You can use it to illustrate cold water or food, for example. This can serve as a visual warning for an eager toddler trying ice cream for the first time. You can also use it before you go outside for a snowy adventure—even if it's just to your car for a drive to grandma's house in winter. You can even create an opportunity for introducing this sign with a small bowl of chilly water on her high chair.

Cook

Hold one hand flat, palm up, and make flipping motions on it with the other hand, as if you were flipping over a pancake or an omelet for breakfast.

Quick Tip

Cooking may be something your child sees you do often, so if he shows interest or curiosity oblige him with the sign. As your child grows he may want to help you cook as well (such as adding ingredients to a mixing bowl), so this may be a fun activity not only for him to see you do but for him to do as well.

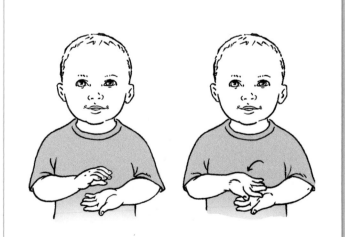

Cook

Cry

To sign cry, track pretend tears rolling down your face with your index fingers.

Cry

Quick Tip

A good way to introduce "cry" is to await the opportunity. Ask him, "Are you crying? What is wrong?" while showing the sign. He will soon associate the sign with crying and can apply it to those around him as well. It can be a good tool for him to have to explain how he's feeling or what others around him are doing.

Cup

Cup

Keeping one hand flat, curve your other hand into the shape of a "C" and tap it a few times onto the flat hand. It looks like the shape of a cup, which should help you remember this one.

Quick Tip

Using "cup" in context may help him with the transition from breast or bottle to cup and may help him differentiate between the two.

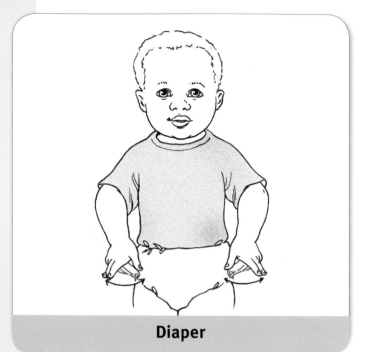

Diaper

Diaper

With the thumbs of both hands resting on your waist, tap the first two fingers of each hand together with the thumbs. Think of the tape on disposable diapers to help you remember this one.

Quick Tip

Your baby might easily confuse this sign with the one for "change." You might choose to use just one while he is still young and introduce the other as he grows, or you can use both from the beginning. As with all signs (and spoken words as well) he will be able to differentiate between the signs as he matures.

Dirty

Hold your hand under your chin and wiggle your fingers.

Quick Tip

This sign might not look like it means "dirty," but you will definitely be reminded of it when you learn the sign for "pig" because they are very similar. This sign can be used to communicate about several different situations your baby might find himself in—such as getting dirty knees from crawling around the house, playing outdoors, getting ready for a bath, and having a dirty diaper!

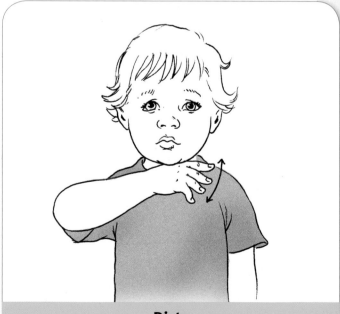

Dirty

Down

This is an extremely easy sign to learn, do, and remember—simply point downward a few times.

Quick Tip

This sign can also be applied to several different situations. Your baby might use it to let you know that he wants "down" from his high chair or swing. You also might use it yourself when he is a bit older to let him know he needs to sit down in a chair.

Down

Dress

This sign is similar to clothes—the hands brush down your torso from your chest.

Quick Tip

You might use this instead of "clothes" if you're looking for a verb to describe your activity. You can say, "Let's get dressed!" as you pull her clothes out of her dresser.

Dress

Dry

Take your index finger and move it from one side of your chin to the other.

Dry

Quick Tip

This is an excellent sign that has many uses. You can sign it if you are drying dishes, but it can be more useful if your baby has just come out of the bath.

Fall Down

Keep one hand flat, palm up, and make a little person with your two fingers, standing on your other palm. Let this person "fall down," and you have a very useful sign.

Fall Down

Quick Tip

When babies learn to pull themselves up, and then walk, they often fall down, and most often the falls are not serious. Make the most out of every opportunity she presents you with. Once your baby learns this sign it might actually reduce the fear that often results from a fall. If she can tell you that she "fell down," she might concentrate more on the sharing than on the fall itself.

Hat

Hat

Tap your head with your flattened hand a few times. This indicates your head and what you wear on it!

Quick Tip

Take advantage of the situation whenever you or your baby wears a hat. Put her in front of a mirror while she wears a hat and sign it behind her. Gather a collection of different hats for her to try on—she will get a real kick out of it, and hopefully this will spur her on to learn the sign.

Hear

Tap your ear with your index finger.

Quick Tip

Whenever you hear an unusual or loud noise, say, "What's that I hear?" as you sign "hear." After your baby picks this sign up you may be amazed at the noises that he hears. It's a great way to get a glimpse into your child's world.

Hear

"Our baby's favorite signs are everything she can sign, but the one sign she uses all the time is 'help.' She signs so much it's a second language. She even signs when playing with her dolls. It's adorable."

—Renee, mother of twenty-two-month-old Arianna

Help

With your palms flattened and facing inward, tap your chest twice. (Note: This sign has been adapted from ASL to make it easier for a baby to sign.)

Quick Tip

Whenever you see that your baby is frustrated, step in, but not before asking him if he needs help. Pair this with the "help" sign and you are giving him a useful sign that will hopefully help avert a lot of frustration, tears, and possibly even tantrums.

Help

Hot

Put your hand to your mouth and then put it down quickly, as if you had tasted a bite of hot food and had to take it away.

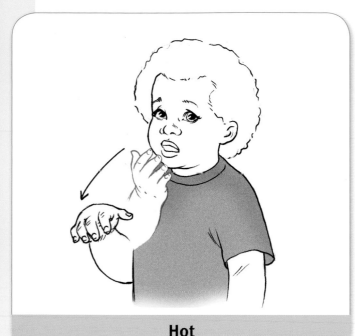

Hot

Quick Tip

This sign is important for safety's sake. Teaching your baby the sign for "hot" will help you not only instill a warning system for a potentially dangerous situation but will help your baby let you know if something is too hot for her. You can use "hot" for the weather, water, the stove, hot food, or anything else that may be too warm for her.

Hungry

Move your cupped hand down your chest from the bottom of your chin. Think of how food travels from your mouth to your stomach and you've got it!

Hungry

Quick Tip

Use this sign when asking, "Are you hungry?" when your baby is displaying signs of wanting to eat.

Hurt

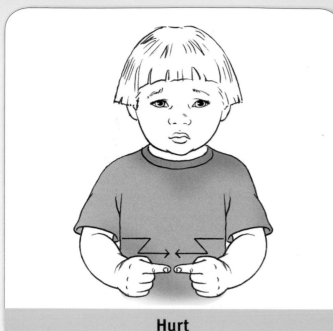

Hurt

Tap your two index fingers together a few times. This sign can be made generically, in front of your body, or over the site of the pain.

Quick Tip

This is an extremely valuable sign. To teach this sign, seize any opportunity that you can. If you see your baby fall, or bump his arm on a table, or bonk himself in the head with a toy, sign "hurt." You can also sign this if you accidentally hurt yourself.

In

In

Put the fingers of one hand into your other hand.

Quick Tip

This sign can be used in play and illustrated by putting toys in a container. Or, you can use it when you are going into your house or getting in your car.

Medicine

Rub the flattened palm of one hand with the middle finger of your other hand—think of the mortar and pestle method of crushing tablets.

Medicine

Quick Tip

Sign this when you administer medicine. Your baby may eventually get to the point where she requests pain medicine if she has a headache, for example, or if she is in pain because of teething.

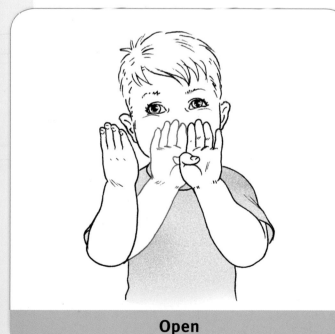

Open

Open

Hold both hands up, palm side out, and move one as though it's a door opening.

Quick Tip

You can use this sign to describe the doors in your home, and your baby may use it as she grows to request that a door be opened for her!

Out

This sign is the opposite of the sign for "in." Pull the fingers of one hand out of your other hand.

Quick Tip

This sign might come to have many uses for you and your baby. She may use it to indicate she'd like to go outside, or that she'd like to get out of her high chair (similar to how she might use "down").

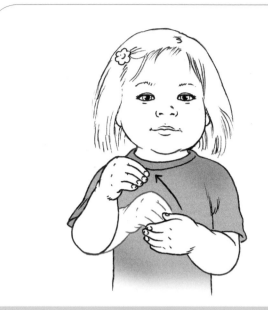

Out

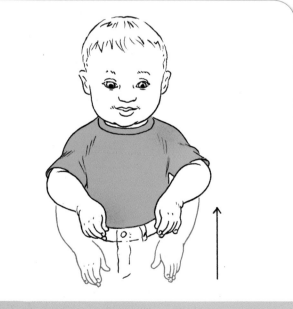

Pants

Pants

Using both hands, flattened and facing one another, move them downward two times, each indicating the legs of a pair of pants.

Quick Tip

This sign should be easy to remember, since it's on the lower part of your body, just like pants themselves. But be alert to the possibility that your baby may sign it on his shirt first!

Shirt

Make a pinching motion near your right shoulder—you can actually pinch your shirt to illustrate it further.

Quick Tip

This sign should be easy to remember, as it shows the material of a person's shirt. You can use this sign as you dress your baby or get dressed yourself.

Shirt

Shoes

Make a fist with each hand and tap them together on the thumb side.

Quick Tip

If you remember *The Wizard of Oz* you might remember this sign—think of how Dorothy was instructed to tap the heels of her ruby red slippers together and you will make this connection! This sign is easily made but be sure to keep the context in mind. This sign can be confused with other signs that are made with a similar motion—"more" and "hurt" are two I can think of right off the top of my head—so take notice of what is going on with your baby at the moment that he makes the sign.

Shoes

Sick

With one hand on the forehead and the other on your belly, make small circular motions with each middle finger.

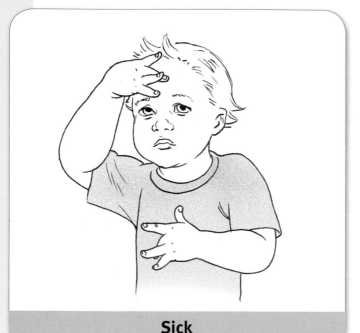

Sick

Quick Tip

Don't forget to have an unhappy expression on your face for this sign. It will help convey the meaning to your baby. You don't have to wait for your baby to become sick to introduce this sign, either. If a family member falls ill, share this with your baby. It's particularly important if the person is a family member he plays with often, so that you can explain why he or she is unable to play that day.

Sleep

Splay all of your fingers, and starting from the top of your head, move them down your face while closing your fingers. Shut your eyes at the end to further illustrate sleeping.

Quick Tip

Use this sign when talking about sleep itself as opposed to your baby's bed. You might focus on other people sleeping, or cartoon characters, or his stuffed animals.

Sleep

Socks

Extend each index finger, put them together, and point downward while rubbing the sides of your fingers together.

Quick Tip

This sign may manifest itself in a variety of ways from the hands of your baby before she gets the proper amount of manual dexterity required to make the sign the correct way. Be sure to acknowledge her efforts and repeat the sign back to her the right way.

Socks

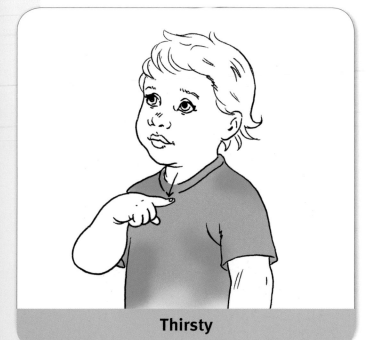

Thirsty

Thirsty

Rub your index finger down your throat. This sign reminds me of what happens when you take a drink—it goes down your throat!

Quick Tip

This sign is great for asking whether your child needs a drink. "Are you thirsty?" you may ask, and then follow that up with the sign for "drink." This might be a sign that you wait to use until she is older—well after she's mastered the sign for "drink."

Toilet

Shake your "T" hand back and forth. The initial reminds me of the word it stands for. See Chapter 9 for how to sign the letter "T."

Quick Tip

This sign is an excellent sign to introduce even before your child begins potty training. It is also a sign that is especially useful when at the store or at the playground.

Toilet

"We home school our Beth now and she enjoys language and the arts. We still use signs like 'potty' (in a public place where saying, 'I am going to use the bathroom' would be an attention-getter)."

—Rayne, mother of seven-year-old Beth

Up

This sign is as simple as the sign for "down"—simply point up a few times.

Quick Tip

Use this sign for the opposite of what you might use for down—for example, when you put her in her high chair, say, "Let's get up in your chair!" And be sure to pair it with "down" when she gets down, as she'll be able to pick it up easier.

Up

Wash Hands

Wash Hands

Simply rub your hands together for this sign, as if you were washing them under a faucet.

Quick Tip

When you first introduce this sign, your baby may not be washing his hands yet. Use it before you wash your hands so that as he grows and learns to wash his own hands it may be easier to pick up.

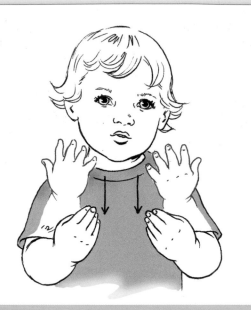

Wet

Wet

The motion for this sign is similar to the sign for "sleep" except that you use both hands in front of your body (instead of at your face).

Quick Tip

This sign is a great one to pair with "dry." If your baby loves to play with water, either in the tub or out, be sure to demonstrate how she gets "wet" and what you do to "dry" her off.

Window

Stack both flat hands, facing your body, one on top of the other, and open your "window" by raising and then lowering your top hand.

Quick Tip

In addition to pointing out the actual window to your baby as she peers through it, use this sign when opening and closing your windows—either at home or in your car. Before long your baby may surprise you by signing "window" if she wants a window open! This is a good sign to pair with both "open" and "close" as she grows.

Window

Activity

"This is the way we . . ."

This activity requires no special materials but is an excellent way to introduce many signs that are based on needs or routine.

For example, if you wanted to teach the sign for "wash hands," you'd sing:

> This is the way we wash our hands
> Wash our hands
> Wash our hands
> This is the way we wash our hands
> All day long

You can teach any other signs in this chapter this way as well. You might have to demonstrate the signs yourself, or you can possibly get your baby involved if she's old enough and able.

Some good ones to start with:

- "Brush teeth"
- Take a "bath"
- "Change" your "diaper"
- "Clean" the dish
- Take our "medicine"
- Get "down" from our chair
- Go to "bed"
- Put on our "shoes"
- Put on our "clothes"

Chapter

2

Animals

Animals Are All Around

Animals can be extremely exciting—and motivating—to babies and toddlers. Enlarging your animal sign language vocabulary is an excellent way to not only have animal signs ready for when your baby requests them but also to allow you to actually create positive signing situations.

Animals surround your baby even if you don't have pets in your home. Animals appear on her clothing, blankets, dishes, and even in the form of stuffed animals. There will be plenty of opportunities to introduce new animal signs to your baby as you go about your daily routine, and as animals are often extremely exciting to your baby it will be a really good motivation for her to *want* to learn new signs.

Be on the lookout for when your baby lets you know that she would like to learn a new animal sign. Does she show delight when she sees a photo of a baby monkey? Oblige her with a rousing display of monkey fun—the sign paired with some monkey hooting can be good for a great laugh and will spark your baby's imagination and desire to sign it to you next time.

"Griffin loves signing animals. Once he got 'cat' and 'dog' down, he always did them when he saw them in books, real life, or stuffed. So we started teaching him the signs of the other animals that appear in his favorite books. Now he goes through certain books that have a cat or mouse on every page, points to the animal, and does the sign. He does not really seem to care what else is on the page."

—Laurinda, mother of fifteen-month-old Griffin

Creating Opportunities

Teaching animal signs will give you loads of possibilities for creating signing opportunities. Instead of teaching signs that are solely based on her physical needs or daily routine, teaching animal signs may encourage your baby to sign because animals make fun noises, move in interesting ways, are colorful, or simply because your baby thinks they are downright cool.

This potential excitement can be a great boon to you in your signing adventures. Think of it this way: Once your baby discovers how his needs are met by communicating with you, he will be that much more excited to learn additional signs. The possibilities are only limited by his interest and your signing vocabulary! Beef up your vocabulary now and keep this book handy so you can provide the proper sign to your child when he requests it.

Signing opportunities are easy to find when using animal signs. Use what you already have in your baby's world. For example, his favorite book might feature jungle animals. Instead of waiting for him to give you a cue that he is interested in learning a sign, point out a particular animal, say its name loud and clear, and show him the sign for it several times. Accompany this with the animal's noise and you might easily pique your baby's interest. Take advantage of this interest when visiting a farm or zoo and his vocabulary may really take off!

Sounds & Signs

Combining animal sounds with their sign is a really fun and easy way to increase the interest factor of the sign. The more dimensional your communication is, the more interesting it may be to your baby.

Alligator

Create a "mouth" with both hands, joined at the wrist, and snap it shut a few times.

Quick Tip

A fun way to incorporate "alligator" is to try to "bite" your child with the sign. She will probably think it's hysterical, and the added bonus of the tactile stimulation combined with a game will encourage her to sign it back to you.

Alligator

Animal

Let your fingertips rest on your chest as your hands move back and forth. You may want to wait until your child is a bit older and has mastered a few specific animal signs before attempting this one.

Animal

Quick Tip

You can remember this sign if you picture an animal running around. (It reminds me of the breathing motions of an animal.)

Bear

Quick Tip

This sign may start out looking more like your baby is hugging herself. Try to keep that in mind while you're waiting for her to sign it back.

Bear

With your arms crossed in front of your chest, make clawing motions toward yourself.

Bird

With your index finger and thumb, create a beak at your mouth, opening and closing it a few times. This sign is an easy one to remember because it reminds you of a bird's beak.

Bird

Quick Tip

Take full advantage of all birds you see, and show your baby this sign whether you've just come across the family pet or a cardinal.

"Jacob learned 'bird' after we repeatedly sang 'Rockin' Robin' to him in the car, doing the sign to every 'tweet/twiddleydiddleydeet' in the song."

—Jennifer, mother of sixteen-month-old Jacob

Bug

Bug

With your thumb on your nose, move your first two fingers up and down a few times.

Quick Tip

Your moving fingers might remind you and your baby of a bug's antennae.

Butterfly

Cross your hands in front of you, join your thumbs together, and flap your hands.

Quick Tip

Fortunately, this sign looks just like a butterfly so it's easy to remember. "Butterfly" is a fun sign because your little one will find real butterflies beautiful and eye-catching. Butterflies have always caused a lot of excitement around here, especially when we were lucky enough to witness the metamorphosis of a Monarch butterfly outside our front door.

Butterfly

"We would sit out in the grass and whatever caught her eye, I would sign it…like airplanes, butterflies, grass…soon my husband, my daughter, and I knew over fifty signs by the time Beth was a year old."

—Rayne, mother of seven-year-old Beth

Camel

Show the camel's two humps by outlining them with your hand.

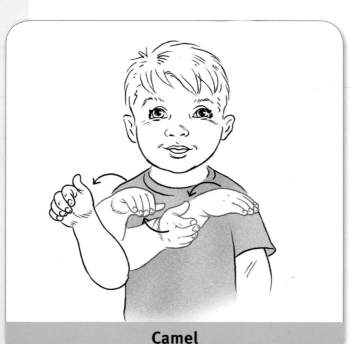

Camel

Quick Tip

Your baby may create this sign in the beginning by a generalized waving or bumping of one, or even two, arms.

Cat

Using one or two hands, stroke your whiskers!

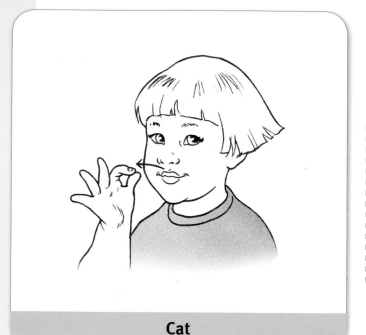

Cat

Quick Tip

Cats are extremely popular with all sorts of people, including small children. Once your baby shows interest in a cat—live or not—be sure to call his attention to it and encourage him to sign it by talking about the cat with your child.

Chicken

Chicken

Begin as though you were going to sign "bird," and then take your beak down to your flattened other hand (the "ground") and peck at the ground.

Quick Tip

As with the spoken word, this sign can refer to the animal *or* the food item.

Dog

Quick Tip

A common approximation that many babies will do for this sign is to pat another area of the body—such as the chest or their other arm—before they refine the sign and do it how you do it.

Dog

You sign "dog" by patting your thigh a few times. An acceptable alternative would be to include a snap after the thigh pat. This sign is easy to remember because it's what many of us naturally do when we would like to call our dogs to our sides—so watch out if there are dogs nearby!

Cow

Twist your "Y" hand near your temple. This can be done with either one or both hands. See Chapter 9 for how to sign the letter "Y."

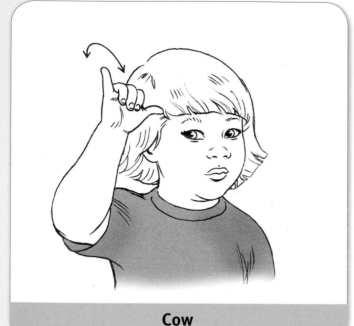

Cow

Quick Tip

This sign immediately brings to mind the horns of a cow. Since cows can be pretty interesting to a young child, this is a good one to pair with a hearty "moo" from mom and dad.

Duck

This sign is very similar to "bird" with the exception that you use your first two fingers instead of just the index finger.

Quick Tip

To help your child remember the difference between "duck" and "bird," make the sounds for each while signing to him. Watch for your baby's interpretation and use other clues to what he may want to share with you. These two signs will often look exactly the same, particularly when your baby starts signing them to you.

Duck

Elephant

Outline the shape of an elephant's trunk by demonstrating a downward curving movement with your hand, starting at your nose.

Quick Tip

Be sure to trumpet like an elephant when signing this for a fun time!

Elephant

Fish

Fish

This sign is easy—make your hand "swim" in the water!

Quick Tip

You can use one hand by itself or pair it with the other hand's fingers resting on the dominant hand's lower palm. As with "chicken," this sign can signify the animal or the food.

Frog

Place your hand under your chin, and flick your first two fingers out a few times.

Quick Tip

This sign reminds me of a frog's kicking legs, and a round of loud "ribbits" will not only make this sign a lot of fun but will help her remember it.

Frog

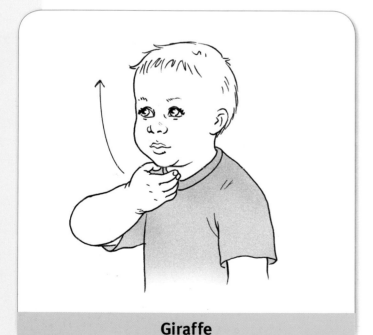

Giraffe

Giraffe

Starting at your neck, raise your hand in the shape of a "C" above your head. See chapter 9 for how to sign the letter "C."

Quick Tip

This sign is another one that is easy to remember, as it shows the shape of a giraffe's long neck.

Goat

Start with a fist at your chin and, as you move it up to your forehead, change it to a "V." See Chapter 9 for how to sign the letter "V."

See Chapter 9 for how to sign the letter "V."

Quick Tip

This sign is an entertaining one. You can remember it by thinking of a goat's beard and then his horns. You might make great use out of this sign the next time you and your child visit a place where goats abound, such as a petting zoo.

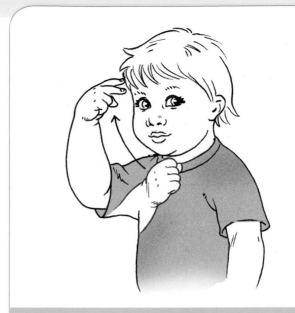

Goat

Gorilla

All you have to do to sign "gorilla" is pound or thump your chest—as a territorial gorilla might do in the wild!

Quick Tip

This sign can be a pretty exciting one to your child and is easy to do, so if your child is a bit older and has several signs under her belt already, she probably will pick it up rather quickly.

Gorilla

Hippo

Make a "Y" handshape with both hands and tap the thumbs and pinky fingers of each hand to their mates on your other hands. Think of a hippo's mouth when you do this sign. See Chapter 9 for how to sign the letter "Y."

Hippo

Quick Tip

When your baby signs this back to you, you might confuse it with "alligator," so keep an eye on what she may be trying to share with you. For example, look at what is in the book she is looking at. Is there a stuffed hippo nearby? Keeping the context of the situation and communication in mind will help you to more accurately read what she is trying to sign.

Horse

With your thumb on your temple and your first two fingers pointing up, make your "ear" flick a few times.

Quick Tip

The sign should remind you of what you might see a horse do when he is confronted by flies out in the pasture.

Horse

Kangaroo

Hold your hands up in front of your body and bounce your hands forward a few times, which reminds me of the action of a kangaroo hopping. Make sure to hold all your fingers together, with your whole hand pointing downward.

Kangaroo

Quick Tip

This sign can be easily turned into a game of follow-the-leader for an older child!

Lion

Lion

Starting from your forehead, go up and over your head, signifying the male lion's beautiful full mane. Your hand shouldn't touch your head.

Quick Tip

Your baby may make her "lion" sign in many different ways. Lauren always did it with a sort of diagonal motion instead of the front-to-back motion that the sign requires. As long as *you* keep showing her the sign the correct way, she will soon alter the way she does it, similar to how she will eventually learn to pronounce words correctly.

Lizard

Let your finger crawl up the back of your arm! Make an "L" hand-shape with your dominant hand and move it up toward your elbow as the finger bends and wiggles. See Chapter 9 for how to sign the letter "L."

Lizard

Quick Tip

The hand shape indicates the first letter of lizard and the motion might remind you of a lizard's movement.

Monkey

Monkey is one of our all-time favorite signs, and it may become your child's as well. Simply scratch your armpits a few times. It sounds funny but can be hysterical when your child tries it out.

Quick Tip

Be sure to hoot like a monkey when you sign this to guarantee a surefire hit!

Monkey

Mouse

Flick the end of your nose with the index finger of your dominant hand.

Quick Tip

To help you remember this sign, think of a mouse's twitching nose.

Mouse

Penguin

Penguin

With your hands down and your arms at your sides, slightly bent at your elbow, move your body like a penguin does—first one shoulder goes up, and then the other.

Quick Tip

This sign should remind you of the way a penguin walks, or waddles.

Pig

With your hand under your chin, flap your fingers up and down.

Pig

Quick Tip

This sign may not *look* like a pig, but when you think of the sign for "dirty" you might make the connection. The two signs are so similar and for good reason—pigs love to wallow in the mud, and can be quite dirty at times. This sign is another great one to match up with its accompanying sound, so "oink" away.

Rabbit

With both hands facing back-wards, place them on either side of your head and flick the "ears" (your first two fingers) a few times. The sides of your hands—where the little fingers are—should be placed to the sides of your head while doing this sign.

Rabbit

Quick Tip

This sign looks like a rabbit's ears, so it's pretty easy to remember.

Sheep

Make shearing motions from the wrist to the elbow with on the inside of one arm with the opposite hand.

Sheep

Snake

Make the shape of a "V" with your index and middle finger. Starting from your mouth, move your "V" handshape in a spiral or wavy motion away from your body.

Snake

Spider

Put one hand over the other and wiggle all of your fingers as your hands, together, shift sideways.

Quick Tip

Spiders may be fascinating—or scary—to babies and young children. Be sure to follow her cues as you point out and introduce her to her world. Signs are as useful in new or frightening situations as they are in fun and exciting situations. Signing gives so much power to a pre-verbal child, and by signing with her you are giving her a great gift.

Spider

Squirrel

Squirrel

Put your hands together and tap two "V" handshapes together to sign "squirrel." See Chapter 9 for how to sign the letter "V."

Quick Tip

If you picture a squirrel chomping on a walnut you can relate it to this sign, which looks like the teeth of a certain bushy-tailed neighborhood rodent.

Tiger

Quick Tip

This sign illustrates the stripes on a tiger's face. Lauren, my daughter, approximated this sign by going *down* her cheeks instead of *across*, but since I recognized her sign because she used all of her fingers, I could tell what she was trying to share. Roaring is a great thing to do with this sign!

Tiger

Brush both cheeks from your mouth to your ears, with all of your fingers spread, in a single motion.

Turtle

Cover your dominant hand with your other hand, keeping your thumb out, and wiggle your thumb.

Turtle

Zebra

Show stripes on your torso with both hands, which signifies the stripes on a zebra's body.

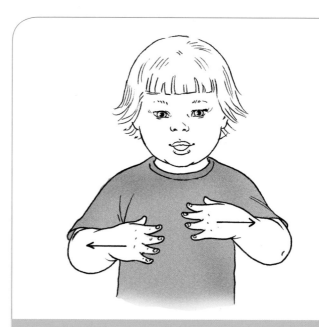

Zebra

Activity

Magazine Zoo

Here is an easy activity that you can do with your child to help increase her animal sign language vocabulary.

Make It

1. To start, go through the magazines with your child. Choose photos of different types of animals and cut them out. You can either let your baby point out what she's interested in or you can pick.

2. Cut out each animal.

3. Glue one on each index card, or, if you have many small photos of one type of animal, you can put several on one. Try not to mix the animal types on each "page." You can use one side or both sides if you wish.

4. Label each page.

5. Slip each index card into a baggie, and seal.

6. When you have several (try for ten or so), line them all up so they are all facing the same way and staple along the sides, as you would if you were making a book.

7. **Most important**—cover the staples with tape. As stated above, strong, wide packaging tape works best, or some other tape that cannot be easily peeled off and become a dangerous choking hazard.

You will need:

- **Magazines!** Nature magazines, conservation magazines, pet care magazines, or any magazine that has photographs or illustrations of a variety of animals, either in advertisements or featured articles.
- **Index cards** (you can use either white cards or colored—you choose)
- **Glue** or glue stick
- **Scissors**
- **Tape** (regular tape will do but strong, 2" (5 cm)-wide packaging tape will work best)
- **Stapler**
- **Locking plastic baggies**
- **Marker**

Play with It

Make sure that you know the sign for each animal and show the book to your child as you would any other book. Use my suggestions for maximum fun—say the animal's name, show her the sign, and make the animal noise if you want to!

Be sure to supervise your baby each time she plays with the book, and check beforehand that the tape is not coming loose and the staples are not exposed. *Have fun!*

Chapter

3

Fun and Nature

Hanging Out
and Having Fun

This chapter is full of signs that you will be able to introduce during fun times—when you attend parties, explore your neighborhood park, look out your child's window at nature, play with toys, and many other opportunities. The objects and activities these signs represent, just like the animal signs in the previous chapter, may be extremely motivating for your baby, and she may pick up the signs quickly. Of course, she also may not be as interested in these signs as others, so feel free to check back in when she does show an interest.

Exploring the outdoors—either through a window or actively playing in it—is often entertaining for babies and parents alike, particularly if you live in an area that experiences the changing of the seasons. This means that every few months you may have a new crop of signs to teach. For example, in the spring you will be able to teach "flower" and "rain"; in the summer you might have more opportunities to teach "sun," "outside," and "park"; in the fall you may focus on "wind" and the colors of the leaves; and in the winter you could show your baby the signs for "cold" and "snow."

Baby's favorite toys (or even *your* favorites!) may become objects of interest and evolve into easy signs for her to pick up. Keep your eye out for what your baby seems to show the most interest in and focus on learning those signs.

Ball

Ball

Tap all of your widespread fingers of one hand together with all of the fingers of the other hand.

Quick Tip

This sign is easy to remember because it looks like what it is—you are making the shape of a ball. Balls are often one of baby's favorite toys, so this might be an early sign that you introduce to him when you start out signing.

Camera

Simply pretend you are taking a photo with an imaginary camera. Hold both hands up to your face, with your index fingers and thumbs forming half of a square, and move the index finger of your right hand up and down as though pressing the shutter.

Quick Tip

If your family is anything like my family, there are lots of photos taken of your baby and lots of photo opportunities. Simply sign "camera" when it's out and ready!

Camera

Book

Book

Put both hands together and then fold them open and out, as if your hands were a book and you were opening it.

Book

Quick Tip

This is another sign that is easy to remember and also may be one of baby's favorites. You can use it right before you visit the bookshelf or when you notice that your baby is paging through a book by herself. Asking, "Do you want to look at a book?" while signing "book" is the easiest way to teach this sign.

Clouds

Clouds

Let your hands outline the general shape of clouds using big broad movements.

Quick Tip

It may be a while before a baby looks up to notice big, fluffy, beautiful clouds, but the bonus is that this is an easy sign for her to reproduce. One of the most amazing things that Lauren did as a young signer (at approximately twenty to twenty-four months) was not only sign "cloud" but then also start signing what she imagined she saw in the clouds. I was blown away to look at her in the backseat, looking out the window and signing "dog," "bird," and "bunny."

Computer

A "C" handshape moves along the forearm with small circular motions. This sign can also be made with a simple back-and-forth motion along the forearm. See Chapter 9 for how to sign the letter "C."

Quick Tip

Kids are using computers earlier and earlier these days, and they also notice mom and dad checking their e-mail on this interesting machine. A young signer may approximate this by rubbing his arm before he refines the sign into its correct form.

Computer

Dance

Make a "person" with your first two fingers in the shape of a "V" and have them "dance" on the flat open palm of your other hand. See Chapter 9 for how to sign the letter "V."

Quick Tip

Since this sign requires the use of two fingers, your baby may "dance" with her whole hand instead of just one person. Continue signing it the correct way and she will eventually refine her signing. Use this sign when you're hanging out, listening to fun music. Invite your baby to "dance" using this sign and whirl her around the room, or show your walker how to get started.

Dance

Doll

With a bent index finger, stroke your nose downward a few times.

Quick Tip

This sign is easy to do but may be a little hard for you to remember. Perhaps think of a cute button nose of a doll! This sign might be very motivating for your baby so be sure to show it to her as soon as you notice her interest.

Doll

Draw

With your pinky finger, "draw" on the palm of your other hand.

Draw

Quick Tip

This sign looks exactly like what it is—drawing! Use it to engage your baby before you bring out his crayons and paper, and sign it occasionally while he's actually drawing. You can also use it for your own drawing. Be sure to say, "Look, Daddy is drawing too!"

Drums

To sign "drums," simply pretend to beat imaginary drums in front of your body with both hands.

Quick Tip

Whether you have toy drums or prefer to scatter pots and pans around the kitchen and let your baby loose with a wooden spoon, this sign will definitely come in handy to a noise-loving baby and her parents. It's an easy sign to remember and do.

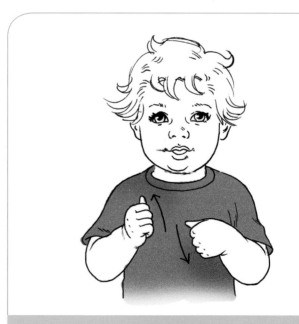

Drums

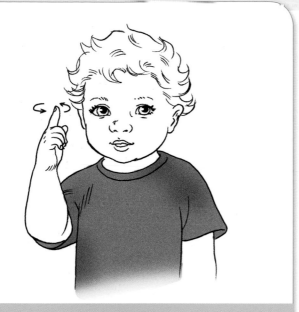

Fan

Fan

To sign "fan," simply twirl your index finger beside your head.

Quick Tip

This might be an early sign for your baby, as many babies love to lie on the floor and gaze up at the ceiling fans (if you have them in your home). If your baby isn't looking at you, you can make the sign just within his line of sight. You can also use this sign for other fans as well, and it can be particularly useful to warn your baby away from fans that may be on his level.

Flower

Put the fingers and thumb of one hand together and move it from one side of your nose to the other.

Quick Tip

This sign is a pretty popular one. Flowers are in so many places—outdoors, in pots on the windowsill, on clothing, and in books and magazines. There are so many places to learn and teach this sign, and the variety of colors and shapes will probably be very interesting to your baby. In nice weather, take advantage of natural beauty as you visit a park or play in your yard.

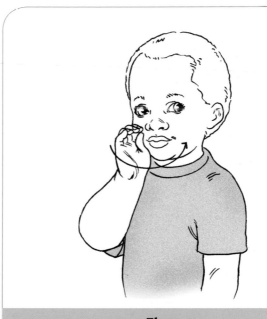

Flower

Gift

Gift

Hold both arms up near your body, with your hands in the "X" handshape, and lower them in an arch. See Chapter 9 for how to sign the letter "X."

See Chapter 9 for how to sign the letter "X."

Quick Tip

This sign can be remembered by its motion—it looks like you are giving a gift to someone. This sign can help build vocabulary for your baby as you are wrapping a gift for a party or giving him a gift for a holiday. This is a very good sign for you to remember before any gift-giving celebration happens, and you will have the sign all ready to show your baby when he's handed a gift!

Grass

Brush your chin with the heel of your hand a few times with the fingers of that hand pointing up. You might think of an animal eating grass when you sign this.

Quick Tip

I know that my children's first "grass" experience was a very interesting one. Dagan, in particular, acted as though I had sat him down on a porcupine. He immediately wanted to be picked up! Having this sign ready to show your children will benefit them and give them a way to communicate with you about this new strange itchy stuff.

Grass

Jump

This sign is very similar to "dance." The main difference is that here your little person "jumps" instead of making dance moves.

Quick Tip

Show your walker this sign when you jump up and down and see whether you can get her to imitate you. Have her toys "jump" for her and remember—you can show her the sign before or after the action, along with saying the word.

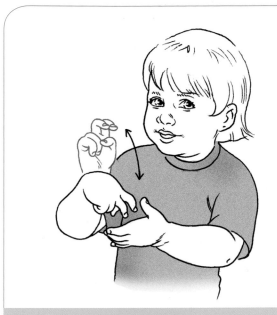

Jump

Key

Key

Using the bent index finger of one hand, "open" a lock on the palm of your other hand.

Quick Tip

We mostly used this sign to talk about our baby keys, but once our signing babies noticed us putting a real key in a lock they were very interested as well. This was one of Corbin's first signs (he really enjoyed his baby keys), so if this is one of your baby's keen interests as well be sure to learn it to show her as soon as the opportunity arises.

Light

Put your thumb and middle finger together and bring both to your chin area. Flick your finger a few times.

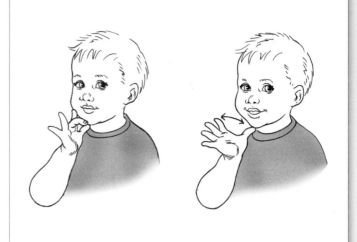

Light

Quick Tip

This sign can also represent something extremely interesting to your baby—the lights! Be sure to sign it as you turn on a lamp or a room's light. You may need to sign it on your baby's face because she may just be too enthralled to look away once it's caught her attention.

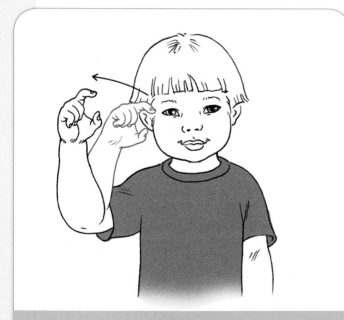

Moon

Moon

Make a "C" with just your thumb and index finger. Starting at your temple, move the "moon" away from your head. See Chapter 9 for how to sign the letter "C."

Quick Tip

If you're traveling at night or your baby notices a moon out his window, be sure to show and talk about this sign. This sign looks like a crescent moon so it's very easy to remember. Since this sign requires the use of a pretty precise handshape, don't be surprised if your baby uses his whole hand instead of just the finger and thumb.

Movie

Both hands are flat; one is facing the signer, the other faces away and, with fingers splayed and pointing up, simply slides back and forth along the thumb side of the other hand. Think of film moving through a projector.

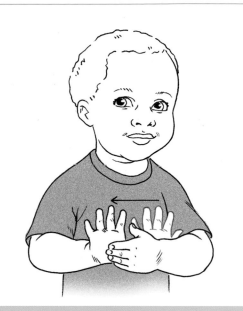

Movie

Quick Tip

Movie time may be a special occasion in your house. It may be exciting to her and this is what makes a sign a good one to teach—something that really stimulates and interests your baby.

Outside

At shoulder level, grasp the air and pull it away from your body.

Quick Tip

Going outside can be thrilling for your baby. There are lots of new sounds and sensations and things to look at. Be sure to sign "outside" before you go out, and if it's too cold or nasty to venture outdoors, you and your baby can look out the window and still discuss the things that are going on out there!

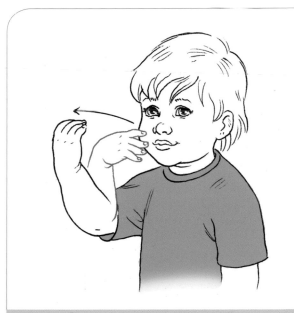

Outside

Party

Party

Swing both "P" hands out in front of your body. See Chapter 9 for how to sign the letter "P."

Quick Tip

This sign is a fun one and since this sign, as others mentioned here, requires the use of pretty specific handshapes, it may be a sign that your baby does in a more vague—or even wild—way. You can use this sign during, or even before, you have a birthday party, and if your child already knows this sign it can be an excellent way to prepare her for a party that you are going to go to.

Phone

"Talk" on a "phone" using your "Y" hand. See Chapter 9 for how to sign the letter "Y."

Quick Tip

This was another of my babies' favorite signs. They loved all phones, play and real—pushing the buttons was too much fun! Your baby may start using this sign in a more general way, such as a closed fist on the side of the face. Despite this, pay close attention to what he's looking at or may want so you can continue to demonstrate it correctly, all the while knowing what he wants

Phone

Piano

To sign "piano," simply pretend to play an imaginary piano in front of your body.

Quick Tip

This is an easy sign to do and remember. You can use it to signify a real piano or a child's electronic version. If your baby loves playing the piano, show this sign to her early on. Look for a generalized sweeping or waving motion first before she shows you the correct finger manipulations.

Piano

Play

Form two "Y" hands and shake them. See Chapter 9 for how to sign the letter "Y."

Quick Tip

This might be a sign that your baby recognizes well before he can sign it back to you. One of my good friends used this sign a lot when her son was small and it always got a great response—he would bounce up and down with a huge grin on his face because he knew it was time to "play." Sign it before you get out a favorite box of toys or when you approach the swing set.

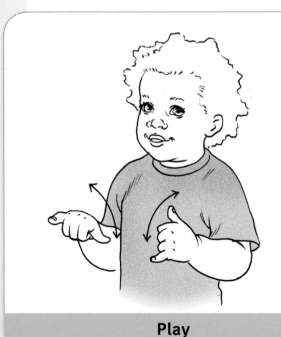

Play

Rain

Spread and bend all of your fingers and wave them up and down a couple of times. This helps illustrate the concept of raindrops falling from the sky.

Rain

Quick Tip

Take advantage of a surprise shower as you play at the park and show your baby the "rain" sign. You can also easily teach this sign watching a rainstorm from indoors. Your baby may want to sign "water," and this is fine too. You could then say (and sign), "Yes! The 'rain' is 'water' falling from the sky."

Read

Make a "V" with one hand and run it up and down the palm of your other hand. See Chapter 9 for how to sign the letter "V."

Quick Tip

Think of the "V" in this sign as a pair of eyes reading a book. You might pair this sign with book for an older child; for example, "Would you like to 'read' a 'book'?"

Read

Slide

Slide

Make an "H" with both hands, one on top of the other (one hand facing the other) and slide them back and forth. See Chapter 9 for how to sign the letter "H."

Quick Tip

Use this sign right before baby goes down the slide, no matter if it's a "real" slide or she's practicing sliding on mommy's legs in the living room. You can also use it to talk about what you're going to do at the playground or what she did that day.

Star

Rub your index fingers together as you point them toward the sky.

Quick Tip

Until your baby starts noticing real stars, be sure to point out stars everywhere else that you see them. Look in books, on store signs, on packages, on clothes, or draw them yourself. This sign is very similar to "shoes" ("shoes" is the same motion, but the fingers point down), so be sure to note the circumstances before you assume she's signing one or the other!

Star

Sun

Make a circular motion to the upper side of your head, then open all your fingers toward your head.

Sun

Quick Tip

Obviously you don't want your child looking directly at the real sun, so make sure to find lots of sun drawings or other examples in everyday life. My kids always liked to sign what they found in the sky—"sun," "moon," "stars," and "clouds"— because it was a lot of fun and all the objects were visibly different.

Toy

Shake both "T" hands back and forth. See Chapter 9 for how to sign the letter "T."

Quick Tip

This sign is very similar to "play"— they have the same movement but use different handshapes. Use this sign when talking about his toys in general. Your baby may confuse or interchange the signs "play" and "toy," but as long as you keep doing the correct sign with the correct spoken word your baby will eventually sort it out!

Toy

Tree

Rest one elbow in your other palm and rotate your hand, fingers spread like the branches of a tree blowing in the wind.

Quick Tip

Like many of the nature signs in this chapter, this sign can be taught either while looking at trees in your yard or photos or drawings of them in books or magazines.

Tree

TV

Signing "TV" is easy for adults—sign a "T" followed by a "V." See Chapter 9 for how to sign the letters "T" and "V."

Quick Tip

While easy for adults to sign, this one can be a challenge for little hands. Just keep showing them the correct handshapes, and they will eventually make them correctly. Before then, look for a bouncing hand or maybe a bouncing "V."

TV

Wind

Swing your hands back and forth, like a breeze is blowing them.

Wind

Activity

Outings!

Here are some fun ideas for making the most out of your outings.

- If you need to water your flower garden, take your baby outside with you, keep her in the shade, and share "yard signs" with her—"outside," "tree," "grass," "flower," "clouds," "wind," and maybe even one you weren't expecting—"rain"!

- For car rides, don't pass up the opportunity to teach the sign for "key," as well as signs that she can look for out the car window, such as "clouds" and "moon."

- Going to a local park? Be sure to teach the "yard signs" mentioned above but also signs for "jump," "play," and "slide."

- When you go for a walk in your neighborhood, look for additional opportunities to introduce new signs to your baby.

- Having a party? Keep in mind the following signs that your baby may be interested in: "dance," "gift," "party," and "light."

- Go on an "indoor outing" and point out what you and your baby see: "book," "computer," "toy," "TV," "piano," "phone," "fan," "camera," "doll," and so on.

Chapter

4

Let's Eat!

Motivation and Routine —Perfect Combo!

Dinnertime is an opportune time for your baby to learn new signs. You learned this back in the beginning when you learned the sign for "milk" when you were either nursing or getting a bottle ready for him.

The easiest way to teach food signs is by showing signs to your baby for foods that he eats on a regular basis (that is, after he is an established solid-food eater). With food signs and a rapidly expanding palate, there is really no shortage of opportunities to teach signs to your baby.

Start with a few foods or drinks that your baby eats every day. Once you and your baby have these learned, expand both of your vocabularies by focusing on foods that he seems to be excited about or that are new to his dinner plate.

Before long you might have the pleasure of experiencing a baby who requests signs for particular food items. One way my signing babies let me know that they needed a sign was by giving me "that look"—it's difficult to describe in words but they simply look at you when confronted by something new or exciting, presenting a sweet, inquisitive air. You'll learn to recognize his curious gaze and be able to supply him with all sorts of food signs after reading this chapter!

"We have started incorporating new signs just on the basis of what seems useful. We taught him some food words like 'drink' and 'eat' and then expanded to more specifics, like 'milk' and 'cheese.'"

—Lynna, mother of seventeen-month-old Luke

Apple

To sign **"apple,"** twist your bent index finger on your cheek.

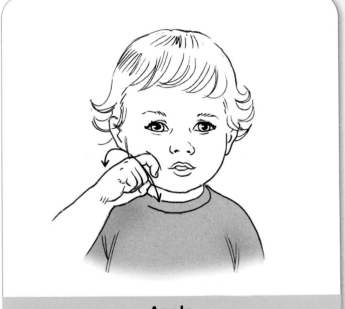

Apple

Quick Tip

This sign is easy to do and is a very popular one, even before baby starts eating real apples. Apples are shiny, colorful, and easy to recognize, so point them out as you grocery shop or flip through books. This sign gets its motion from the act of twisting the stem from an apple. She may approximate this sign by *not* bending her index finger, which may look just like the sign for "candy" if you're not paying careful attention to context!

Fun Fact

American Sign Language (ASL) is a language completely separate from English. It has its own rules for grammar, punctuation, and sentence order.

Banana

Banana

This sign is an easy—and intuitive—one. Simply use one hand to peel the index finger of the other hand (i.e., the banana)!

Quick Tip

This sign requires some precision, so be sure to recognize and respond to your baby's attempts, no matter how indistinct her sign might be. If you mash your own bananas for her to eat, sign "banana" before you peel it as well as while you are mashing it up and serving it to her. This way she will have an easier time making the connection!

Bread

Hold one hand flat against your abdomen and, with your other hand, "slice" a few times on the flat hand.

Quick Tip

This was one of Corbin's earliest signs and if I hadn't been carefully paying attention I would have not had a clue what he was signing at first! He simply held his hands out in front of him and brushed the back of one hand with the other. He loved bread so this was a sign that he picked up on quite easily.

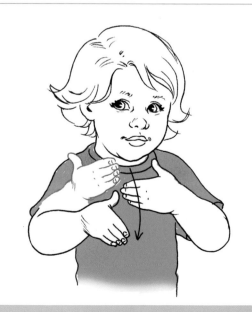

Bread

Cake

Using a "C" handshape, outline the shape of a slice of cake on the opposite palm. See Chapter 9 for how to sign the letter "C."

Cake

Quick Tip

This is a sign for something very fun and exciting. You might first show it to your baby at her first birthday party. Sign it when you bring the cake out as well as while she's smashing it in her hair!

Candy

Twist your index finger by the corner of your mouth.

Candy

Quick Tip

As mentioned before, this sign looks a lot like "apple," particularly when coming from little hands. We saved teaching this sign to Corbin until he was two years old and going on his first Halloween circuit around the neighborhood. He was able to pick up on it quite easily at that age, and of course with how yummy and fun candy is, it made it that much more appealing.

Cereal

You can do this with either one or two hands. Pretend you are scooping cereal out of a "bowl" and bringing it to your mouth.

Cereal

Quick Tip

This is a fairly easy sign to do and remember, so it's a good early one to show to your baby, particularly if she likes eating dry cereal. One thing you might do is get the cereal box out and shake it and then sign "cereal." Hearing the noise will help deepen her association with the sign itself.

Cheese

Join both hands at the heel and twist your top hand from the left to the right, keeping the heels together.

Cheese

Quick Tip

My children have long been cheese lovers, so this was a very popular sign in our house. Like the sign for "bread," their version of this sign may be more generalized than the version you do, but it's a great one to show your own little cheese lover as soon as he shows interest and delight in this food.

Cookie

Pretend to cut out the shape of a round cookie on the palm of one hand with the bent fingers of your other hand.

Quick Tip

Cookies are exciting and fun and may be a sign that your baby picks up pretty quickly. The shape indicates the cookie itself so it may be one that you remember easily, but I've heard of at least one baby simply slapping his hands together when he wanted a cookie!

Cookie

Cracker

Bend your arm and tap the elbow with the fist of your other hand.

Cracker

Quick Tip

This was another very popular sign in our household. Crackers were a very fun food for my babies and teaching them this sign gave them the power to ask for some. Lauren approximated this sign at first by tapping somewhere in the vicinity of her armpit instead of her elbow!

Drink

Drink

This sign is very simple—bring your hand to your mouth as if you were holding a cup and drinking from it.

Quick Tip

This is often one of baby's first signs. You can wait to show it to her until she's using a sippy cup for the first time. Show it to her often—before she gets the cup and even while she's drinking from it.

Eat

Eat

Flatten your "O" hand and touch your lips with your fingertips. See "Signing the Alphabet" to learn to sign an "O."

Quick Tip

This is a very easy sign to remember and for baby to do. He may use one or both hands. Both Corbin and Lauren (my kids) would use *two* hands if they *really* wanted me to know that they wanted to eat!

Egg

Cross both "U" handshapes and move them down and away from one another. See Chapter 9 for how to sign the letter "U."

Egg

Quick Tip

This sign looks like you are actually breaking an egg, so the motion is a pretty fun one to do and to teach. Your baby may get a kick out of watching you break eggs for her pancake, or she may like eating scrambled or hard-boiled eggs for her breakfast. You can also point out the eggs in her farm board books!

French Fries

With your hand in an "F" hand-shape, bounce it to the side two times. See Chapter 9 for how to sign the letter "F."

Quick Tip

While not the healthiest food to feed to a baby, oftentimes toddlers will get exposed to French Fries and may really enjoy learning the sign. It's fun and easy to do—you might think of dipping a fry in ketchup as you show him this sign.

French Fries

Fruit

Twist the "F" handshape by the corner of the mouth. See Chapter 9 for how to sign the letter "F."

Fruit

Grapes

Bounce the bent fingers of one hand down the length of the back of your other hand.

Grapes

Hamburger

Hamburger

Cup your hands together, then rotate and do the same, as if you are forming a hamburger patty.

Quick Tip

Of course this sign is only for toddlers who are meat-eaters, but if yours is a child who loves his burgers you will definitely want to show him this sign.

Ice Cream

Pretend you are eating an ice cream cone—tongue optional! Move your fist in small circles right in front of your mouth.

Quick Tip

This sign is easy to remember because it looks exactly like what it represents —someone eating an ice cream cone. You may want to stick out your tongue like you are licking it—your baby will get a real kick out of that.

Ice Cream

Juice

You can do this sign one of two ways: sign "drink" followed by the fingerspelling of "J," or simply make a wide "J" with your pinky finger. See Chapter 9 for how to sign the letter "J."

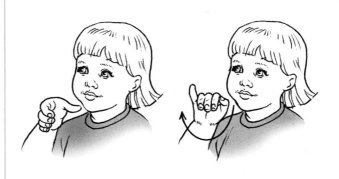

Juice

Quick Tip

We always used the fingerspelling of the letter "J" for juice, although pairing it with the sign for "drink" makes the meaning more clear. Once you introduce juice into your toddler's diet you may find that she loves it, and giving her the means to tell you about it is a wonderful thing to do.

Meat

Pinch the fleshy part of your hand between your thumb and index finger.

Meat

Quick Tip

Since you are pinching the "meaty" part of your hand, this may help you remember this sign. We used it to indicate, for example, sliced deli meat, which Corbin loved from an early age. It is a fairly simple sign to do and remember so if your baby turns out to like meat, you might show him this sign.

Milk

Milk

Using your "C" hand, squeeze it into a fist several times. See Chapter 9 to learn how to make a "C."

Quick Tip

When performing this sign, it should look like you are milking a cow.

Peach

Splay the fingers of your hand on your cheek, then pull your hand away while closing your fingers and repeat this motion.

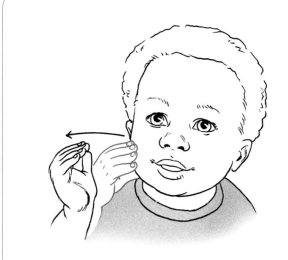

Peach

Quick Tip

This sign looks like you are stroking the soft skin of a peach. You might use it to distinguish between other fruit of the same size and general shape—an apple, for example.

Pear

Pear

Grasp one hand with the other and move it out and away. Imagine one hand trying to "eat" the other!

Quick Tip

This is another good fruit sign to help your baby distinguish between different yummy fruits. You might use this even when she's eating pureed fruit—just point to the picture of the pear on the jar, if you use store-bought baby food, or show her the pears before you make it yourself.

Peas

Hold out the index finger of one hand, and bounce up its length with the bent index finger of your other hand.

Peas

Quick Tip

This sign reminds me of peas in a pod! If your baby likes the fun, round shape of peas—whether he likes eating them is a different matter—be sure to show him this sign. As with pears or other foods that are commonly served as baby food, you can show him the sign for peas while you point to the picture on the jar.

Popcorn

Flick your index fingers against your thumbs as you raise each hand one at a time.

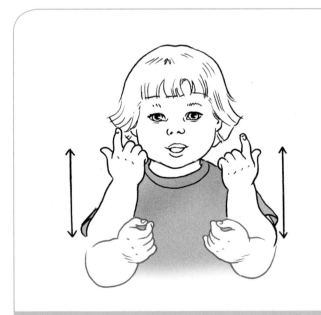

Popcorn

Quick Tip

Obviously popcorn is a treat that you only give once your child has reached a certain age, but once you've introduced it your child may become a huge fan of the salty treat. The motion of the sign reminds me of popping kernels and is a fun sign to do, watch, and learn.

Potato

Tap the back of one hand with the two fingers of a bent "V" handshape. See Chapter 9 for how to sign the letter "V."

Potato

Quick Tip

This sign reminds me of poking a baked potato with a fork. Learning the sign for potato may be done best in moments when your child is actually eating one, but you can still look for drawings of potatoes—or maybe your child has some play mashed potatoes in her play kitchen.

Toast

Toast

Tap both sides of a flat hand with the bent "V" handshape. See Chapter 9 for how to sign the letter "V."

Quick Tip

This is another sign you might reserve until your child is a bit older and can distinguish between regular bread and the toasted variety. The sign itself should help you remember what it is because it shows how a piece of bread is toasted on both sides!

Vegetable

Vegetable

Make a "V" with your hand and alternate touching the area near your mouth with the index finger first, and then rotating your hand to touch it with your middle finger. See Chapter 9 for how to sign the letter "V."

Quick Tip

This sign is similar in function to "fruit" as it's a pretty broad category sign, and you might need to wait until your child is a bit older to introduce it.

Water

Tap the side of your mouth several times with a "W" hand-shape. See Chapter 9 for how to sign the letter "W."

Quick Tip

This sign can be used for much more than drinking water from a cup. You can use it for bath water, for washing hands time, and for puddles of water left over from a rain shower. Since this sign requires a pretty precise "W" your baby may approximate with a "V" or maybe even all of her fingers by her mouth. Any way she does it is correct; just respond appropriately and continue to demonstrate the real version until she gets it.

Water

Activity

Baby Salad Bar

Here is a fun way to introduce a variety of foods and signs to your baby. This activity is best for babies who are already eating table food.

1. Gather a selection of three or four different types of foods. Good examples include bread, cheese, soft fruits (like pears), and cooked vegetables (such as peas), or small pieces of hard-boiled eggs.

2. Place a few pieces of each food into different baby-safe bowls and spread the bowls out in front of her on her high chair tray or on the table.

3. Tell her about her choices, using the signs for each selection. Pretend you are a server at a fine restaurant. Use a lot of variety in your voice to make each item sound fascinating.

4. Whenever your baby grabs her choice, say and sign it again.

> Choose food that is soft and chewable and make sure to cut it into small pieces to avoid choking. Also keep in mind your doctor's suggestions on what foods to avoid at a certain age to steer clear of food allergies.

This way you can not only introduce new foods to your baby but find out what she likes the best. She will let you know which choices she finds the most exciting and palatable.

I suggest giving her the same choices every time you try this activity so she focuses on a few signs at a time; introducing new selections every week or two will help keep her interest.

Grocery Shopping

A simple routine task such as going out to the grocery store can give you many opportunities to teach and reinforce signs. Here are a few suggestions:

- For babies, choose several items on your list that she might be interested in (apples are a good one to start with because they are easy to recognize). As you put the apples in your cart, talk about their shape and color and sign "apple" a few times. Repeat for boxes of crackers, her baby cereal, bottles of juice, cartons of milk...it's only as limited as your vocabulary and your baby's interest!

- For toddlers, make a shopping list for them using drawings or magazine cutouts in addition to the printed words. Talk about and show him the signs for the items you are going to shop for before you step out the door. As you find what you need, show him the sign and have him put it in your cart (if it's not eggs, that is). Encourage him to sign it back to you.

- Once you are back home you can continue to show your baby signs for things that you might find on the food containers. This is a good way to sign not only about food but other things. For example, is there a picture of a cow on your milk carton? Or is there a tree on a box of crackers?

With signing, grocery shopping will never be dull again!

Chapter
5

On the Move

Vehicles and Travel

This chapter is a short one, but it may have some of your baby's future favorite signs within its pages. Boys and girls alike can delight in and play with vehicles of all kinds. My daughter is a perfect example of the notion that cars and trucks are not just for boys—she loves playing with the toy versions, and when she was small she learned the signs for "boat" and "car" early on.

Vehicles are everywhere, and these signs will cover much of what you and your baby may see (or even get in) on a daily basis.

Making Travel Fun

Learning travel signs can help make your daily travels fun or even help when you go on a longer journey.

No matter how you travel, be sure to point out the vehicles around you. If your baby is old enough to ride in a forward-facing car seat, you can take advantage of his position by signing about the cars, trucks, and buses that you see on the road. Visiting an airport? That will make teaching "airplane" easy.

Making it a point to learn new signs before you go on your journey can help your baby focus on something fun and exciting (instead of the baby version of "are-we-there-yet?" that generally manifests itself as fussing or crying).

Fun Fact

American Sign Language (ASL) is said to be the fourth most commonly used language in the United States.

Airplane

Make an "I love you" handshape and "fly" it across in front of you. (You make an "I love you" handshape by extending your thumb, index finger, and pinky.)

Airplane

Bicycle

"Pedal" your fists in front of you.

Quick Tip

This sign is very easy to do and remember because it looks like someone pedaling a bicycle. You can use it for your baby's little toy tricycle or for when he shows excitement at seeing other kids or adults biking around the neighborhood or in the park.

Bicycle

Boat

Cup your hands together and "bounce" your hands forward a few times.

Quick Tip

This sign looks like the shape of a boat, and the movement looks like a boat moving through the waves of an ocean. Boats can be really big so if you see one, do not let that opportunity pass you by! They are bound to make a big impression on your child. Lauren loved to look at pictures of boats, so it was an early sign for her.

Boat

Bus

Put the pinky of one hand together with the index finger of the other hand. Tap them together a few times.

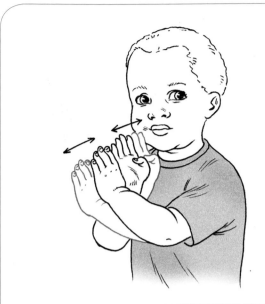

Bus

Quick Tip

This sign reminds me of the opening and closing doors of a bus. School buses in particular are very bright and big so this may be an interesting sign for your child to learn. Show it to him as one passes by your home as you are playing in your yard, or if you drop your older children off at school or they ride the bus themselves there is plenty of opportunity to show it then.

Go

Go

Start with both hands pointing up and then point both forward at the same time.

Quick Tip

Use this sign as you're asking, "Are you ready to go?" If you use it consistently, your baby may not only pick it up quickly but also use it to let you know that she'd like to go somewhere or even go home.

Car

Quick Tip

Ah, cars. Whether you drive one, ride in one, or see one on a daily basis, a car is a simple and fun sign to teach to your baby. It's an easy sign to do and remember and your baby may pick it up easily if she finds cars appealing.

Car

Pretend to "drive" a car by imitating turning a steering wheel.

Stop

Strike your flat palm with the pinky edge of your other hand.

Stop

Quick Tip

This sign has a lot of practical uses. You can use it when you are stopping in a car. You can also use it as an accompaniment to a verbal request that he needs to stop doing something. Facial expression is very important in this last case! Once your child has mastered this sign himself you might be surprised at how he uses it. For example, he might use it if he's not in the mood to hear you sing him a song.

Train

Run the fingers of one "U" hand over the fingers of the other "U" hand. See Chapter 9 for how to sign the letter "U."

Quick Tip

This sign looks like something moving along train tracks so that makes it much easier to remember. We are lucky enough to pass by a whole slew of train tracks on the way to visit family so we have always had a lot of opportunity and time to teach this sign. Looking at books is also a good place to find pictures of trains. Trains are big and noisy, which makes them a good candidate for a baby's interest.

Train

Truck

Make two "T" hands and tap them together a few times. See Chapter 9 for how to sign the letter "T."

Truck

Quick Tip

I have also seen this sign done as "T" hands in a "car" motion—that is, pretend to drive with your "T" handshapes. I think this version is a better one to use as it is more distinct from the "car" version.

Wheels

Using both index fingers, spin to indicate the turning of wheels.

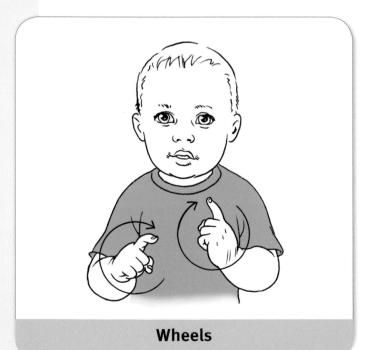

Wheels

Quick Tip

This sign is a fun one to do. Point out the wheels on the vehicles you come across—from airplanes to cars to even trains—and the wheels on her toys as well.

I Spy Vehicles!

With your baby in tow, you can have an educational signing experience using nothing but your vocabulary and the vehicles you see going down the road.

- If you live in a city or on a busy street, set yourself up on your porch or in your driveway. Whenever you see a car, truck, or bus go by, point it out to your baby and show the sign for it. Be on the lookout for airplanes flying overhead as well!

- Vehicle signs can be combined with color signs when your baby gets older for even more fun.

- Do you ever get stuck in traffic? Make the most of it by signing with your baby about the vehicles that are stuck with you!

- For a fun way to teach "boat," share the "Row, Row, Row Your Boat" song. Not only is it simple and repetitive but also it focuses on one sign.

- Add sounds to your vehicle signs for more excitement—vroom vrooms and airplane noises may interest your baby even more!

Chapter
6

People and Places

Let's Go Visiting!

Teaching a baby signs for her favorite family members, places, and other people in her life will allow her to communicate even more.

Learning the signs for her primary caregivers (for example, "mommy" and "daddy") will show you that she may be thinking of someone when they are out of the house (which is a wonderful, reaffirming thing for that person to learn when he or she gets back home).

Involving Family Members

You may be interested in involving other family members in your new way of communication. This can not only increase the consistency that is so important when teaching signing to a young child (if you keep in mind that all participants need to use the same signs), but it can bring joy into family members' lives as well because they will not only be able to communicate with your baby using signs but they will have a much better time understanding the signs your baby makes as well.

Fun Fact

American Sign Language (ASL) changes regionally, just as English is spoken differently in different parts of the country. Ethnicity, age, and gender also affect ASL usage and contribute to its variety.

Aunt

Make small circular motions with your "A" hand a few times. See Chapter 9 for how to sign the letter "A."

Aunt

Boy

Pretend you are grasping the bill of a baseball cap. Open and shut your fingers a couple of times.

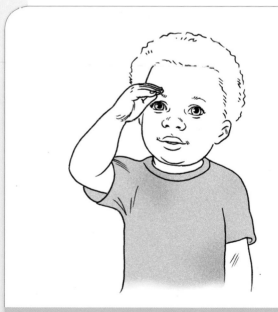

Boy

Baby

Baby

Cradle and rock a "baby" in your arms.

Quick Tip

Babies love babies! Whether the baby is in a book or she sees one in real life she is bound to be very interested. This was one of my signing babies' first signs. Lauren loved it so much that she signed it quite often, even when nursing.

Brother

This sign uses both hands in an "L" handshape. Tap your temple with the thumb of one and then bring it down to join the other "L." See Chapter 9 for how to sign the letter "L."

Quick Tip

This sign combines a sign representing "male" with the sign for "same," which indicates a male member of the same family.

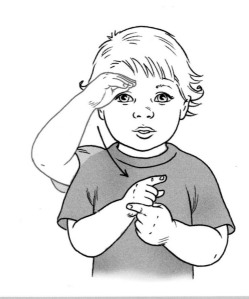

Brother

Cousin

Make circular motions around the jaw line for a female cousin or at the temple area for a male cousin. To indicate "cousin" in general, make the sign in between these two areas.

Cousin

Quick Tip

As with many of the "people" signs, the handshape indicates the first letter of the sign and the placement indicates the sex of the person you are signing about. Doing a generic "cousin" (in between the "male" and "female" areas) is good for talking about all of baby's cousins.

Daddy

Tap your temple with the thumb of your open hand.

Daddy

Quick Tip

A baby's father is so important to her and learning this sign early is a very good idea. Since Dad is a male, we know that it should be made by the temple area. Lauren first did this sign with a closed fist banging on the side of her head but we definitely got the point!

Dentist

Tap your teeth with your "D" hand, then follow by placing both hands, facing one another, in front of your body (this indicates "person"). See Chapter 9 for how to sign the letter "D."

Quick Tip

Before your baby makes his first visit to the tooth doctor, share the word and the sign with him. Learning the sign beforehand may make it more fun and less frightening when you get there.

Dentist

Doctor

Tap your wrist with your "M" hand. This can also be done with a "D" hand. See Chapter 9 for how to sign these letters.

Doctor

Quick Tip

This sign helped Corbin in particular because he had to go to the doctor quite often when he was young. I first taught him the sign when we were in the room with the doctor but you can also show it to your child before you get there. Corbin would use the sign later to share with others that he had been to the doctor.

Family

Start out with both "F" hands joined at the thumb and index finger and make a circular motion to join them on the pinky side. See Chapter 9 for how to sign the letter "F."

Quick Tip

The "F" handshape will help you remember the actual word, and the motion might remind you of a close-knit family—it's actually based on the sign for "group." Use this sign before or during a large family gathering, such as Thanksgiving.

Family

Farm

Trace your jaw line with the thumb of your open hand, from one side to the other.

Farm

Quick Tip

Do you have relatives who own a farm, or do you pass by one every now and then on your daily travels? Maybe your child loves farm books and toys. Use this sign to let her talk about it.

Girl

Trace your jaw line with the thumb of your "A" hand. See Chapter 9 for how to sign the letter "A."

Quick Tip

Try to think of a girl's bonnet and the strings that tie around her chin to keep it secure. This might help you remember this sign. As with "boy," it may be a while before your child notices the difference between boys and girls, but you can help by pointing out examples of each in her favorite books.

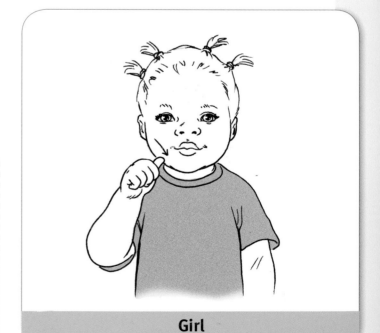

Girl

Grandma

Touch the thumb of your open hand to your chin and **"bounce"** it forward two times.

Quick Tip

This sign is very similar to "mommy" but the extra bounce in it can be thought of to indicate an extra generation.

Grandma

Grandpa

This sign starts with your open hand on your temple and it bounces forward two times.

Quick Tip

Just like with "grandma," this sign is similar to "daddy" but with an extra bounce to indicate an extra generation. Both of the grandparent signs were done early on by my signing babies as a wild bouncing—definitely more than the required two! Lots of practice and seeing me do it correctly helped them get it right.

Grandpa

Home

Touch the side of your mouth and then touch the side of your head with a similar handshape as you sign "eat."

Quick Tip

This sign is easy to remember if you keep in mind that "home" is where you "eat" and "sleep." Your child might use this sign to indicate that she'd like to go home—mine did!

Home

Hospital

Draw a cross shape on the side of your arm.

Quick Tip

This sign reminds me of a uniform a medical professional might wear. Hospitals can be overwhelming and frightening, even if your child isn't the patient. And if he is, be sure to show him this sign.

Hospital

House

Outline the basic shape of a roof and house with your hands.

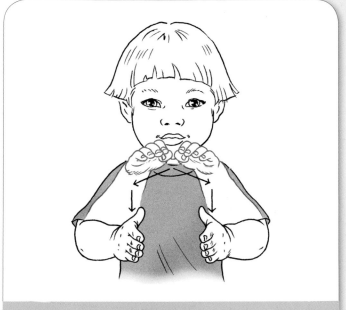

House

Quick Tip

This sign looks like the shape of a house, so that will help you to remember. My kids did take a while before they mastered this one so be sure to acknowledge your baby's efforts, no matter how wild they may look! Point out houses as you go down the street on your walk and in his books.

Library

Library

Make small circular motions with your "L" hand. See Chapter 9 for how to sign the letter "L."

Quick Tip

This sign will not only help you remember the "L" hand sign, but also related signs. As you approach the building, sign "library" and tell her what she will find in there—"books" that she will be able to "read."

Mommy

Tap the side of your chin with the thumb of your open hand.

Quick Tip

This sign looks just like the sign for "daddy" except it indicates a female by being near the chin. You can use it to indicate yourself or others can use it to point you out when you walk in a room.

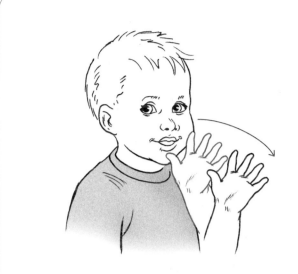

Mommy

Park

Tap your upper chest with a "P" handshape. See Chapter 9 for how to sign the letter "P."

Quick Tip

This may be one of baby's favorite places as well! Sign it to her as you talk about where you are going, and as you approach or pull up in your car, sign it again.

Park

School

Hit the heels of both hands together a few times.

School

Quick Tip

Think of a teacher clapping for attention when you sign this. This sign is very useful if your baby has older brothers and sisters who attend school. Lauren would have a little adjustment period when school was starting back up and would wonder where her brothers were, and by signing it to her she was able to be not quite so worried because she was with me every morning as I dropped them off.

Sister

To sign "sister," make an "L" with both hands. Tap your chin with the thumb of one and then bring it down to your other "L" hand. See Chapter 9 for how to sign the letter "L."

Sister

Quick Tip

This sign is very similar to "brother" with the exception of how it starts—on the chin area as "female" signs are apt to do.

Store

Point both flat "O" hands down, then flick them up and down a few times. See Chapter 9 for how to sign the letter "O."

Store

Quick Tip

This sign is based on the sign for "sell" and for good reason—they are selling what you need! As with all of the "places" signs I share with you, this is a good one to sign as you approach the store itself and to talk about before and after the trip.

Uncle

Make small circular motions around your temple area with a "U" handshape. See Chapter 9 for how to sign the letter "U."

Quick Tip

This sign is similar to "aunt" and "cousin" except it is always done by the temple area and, of course, employs a "U" handshape. This helps you remember that it starts with a "U."

Uncle

Work

Tap one "S" handshape on the back of your other "S" hand-shape. See Chapter 9 for how to sign the letter "S."

Work

Quick Tip

For some reason, I always thought of tapping rocks together to help me remember this—not that many people tap rocks together for their work but it is work in and of itself! I would use this sign when my husband was at work and the baby was curious about where Daddy was.

Zoo

This is signed by fingerspelling Z-O-O. See Chapter 9 for how to sign these letters.

Zoo

Quick Tip

This may belong in the "Advanced" category simply because it requires not one but three letters to be formed, but it's still a valuable sign to introduce to your children when you visit the zoo. They will approximate the best that they can (it may simply be "Z" for a while) but as long as you know the meaning, that's all that matters. Keep demonstrating it correctly and as your baby grows and her fine motor skills mature, she will soon refine her own signing.

Easing Transition in a New Place

Learning the signs for different family members will help your baby make even more of a connection with them and it can also prepare your child for a visit or excursion away from your home. Looking at photo albums and showing signs for "grandma" and "uncle" *before* you go might cut down on any anxiety your baby may feel when going to a new place. This can also be extremely helpful if your baby needs to see a doctor or visit someone in a hospital, or even before picking up a sibling from school.

Chapter
7

Advanced Concepts

Going Beyond the Basics

As your child matures and his vocabulary (and yours!) grows at an astounding rate, he will naturally be more able to grasp new concepts, such as emotions and abstract ideas.

The signs in this chapter cover these concepts and might come in handy in many instances—from diffusing a temper tantrum (e.g., "Do you feel 'mad' or 'sad' right now?") to teaching patience, as well as being able to use new adjectives and prepositions in various situations (as well as funny or unique ones as well).

Signing In a Two-Language Household

One situation some families find themselves in is when they are in a household where there is more than one spoken language used on a daily basis. Many wonder whether introducing sign language is pushing a third language on a child and may be too much for him to handle.

Usually when families sign with their babies they are not teaching the actual language of ASL. It's more like teaching vocabulary from a language as opposed to the sentence structure and grammatical rules that are necessary for a language to function. In essence, signed words can act like a bridge between two spoken languages, which can help everyone involved as long as the same sign is used for the same word. For example, you might sign the ASL version of "big" and "little" while asking, "Do you want the big one or the little one?" as well as "Veus-tu le gros ou le petit?" Keep reading for another way to communicate "big" and "little."

Big

Start with your flat hands close together, and then spread them apart.

Big

Happy

With your flat hand, pat your chest in an upward motion a few times.

Happy

Little

Push both cupped hands toward one another a few times.

Quick Tip

This sign looks just like the opposite of the sign for "big" and can be used or taught similarly. They are a great opposite pair.

Little

Mad

Move a clawed hand toward your face at eye level.

Quick Tip

As with all emotion signs, make sure you have the appropriate expression on your face as you do this sign! Use it when your child is obviously angry (for example, "You look really mad!").

Mad

No

Using your first two fingers and a thumb, snap them open and shut a few times.

Quick Tip

Accompany this sign with a shake of your head and a firm "No!" and it will go far in helping your child understand this meaning. Your child will definitely recognize this sign before he does it himself but the circumstances he uses it in may surprise you! For example, our daughter Lauren loved dogs but she startled easily when ours came indoors, and on more than one occasion I noticed her signing "no" when I went to let Choopie in.

No

Off

Off

Start out with one hand on top of the other and move it quickly "off."

Quick Tip

This sign looks just like what it means, and it's also one that has many, many uses. You can use it to talk about what you are doing (for example, "I'm taking your highchair tray off!") or you might use it to give your child a bit of parental direction ("I need to you get off the dog"). This is another one that is part of a good opposite pair, used with "on."

On

Do this sign the opposite of how you do "off"—place one hand on top of your other hand.

Quick Tip

Use this sign either alone or in conjunction with "off." Teaching it may be as simple as putting a favorite toy "on" a box and then taking it "off" again.

On

Please

Rub your chest with your open hand.

Quick Tip

This has to be one of the cutest, most endearing signs I have ever seen a small child use. Sign it yourself when you request something from your child, and when she asks for something, you can also do the parent's favorite line—"Say please!" My children learned this fairly quickly and soon learned to sign it to their advantage. It is rather hard to say no when your child looks so adorable making such a cute sign.

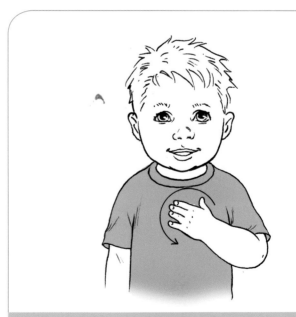

Please

Sad

This sign starts out with both open hands together in front of your face, and then you move both downward.

Quick Tip

Make sure that you have a very sad expression on your face while doing it. Take advantage of any sadness expressed by your child by showing him this sign. It might lead to him signing "sad" instead of crying in the future!

Sad

Sorry

Rub your chest in small circular motions with an "S" hand. See Chapter 9 for how to sign the letter "S."

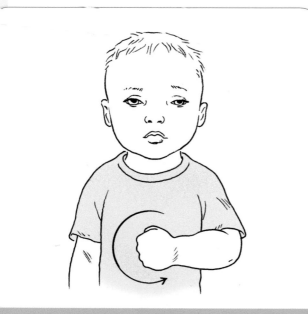

Sorry

Quick Tip

This sign looks very similar to "please" but the handshape will help you remember that it is a different sign. Use it yourself when you make a mistake. Also, use it if your child acts in a manner not befitting the little cherub you know she can be by asking her if she is "sorry."

Thank You

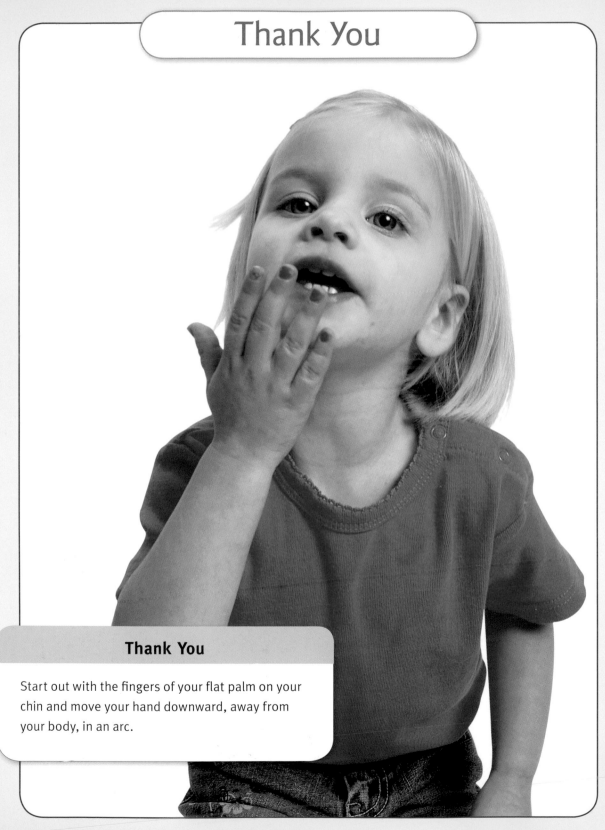

Thank You

Start out with the fingers of your flat palm on your chin and move your hand downward, away from your body, in an arc.

Thank You

Quick Tip

This is another cute sign about manners to teach to your baby. Non-signers often mistake it as a baby blowing kisses, so if you notice your toddler blowing kisses this may be what she is signing! Sign it when your baby hands you something upon your request or does something that you ask.

Wait

Wiggle the fingers of both hands, keeping your dominant hand out in front of the other.

Wait

Quick Tip

This is a useful sign that might be used more by you than your baby. Once your baby understands the concept you can sign it and he will understand that he needs to wait before you can help him.

Want

Pretend you are grasping something and pulling it toward your body.

Want

Quick Tip

This sign is a fairly easy one to do and remember and your baby might find it extremely useful. After all, how many things does a toddler want during an average day? It can be a placeholder for objects that he does not yet know the sign for (but desperately wants) and can also indicate an area in which you need to learn a few more signs!

Where

Move your index finger back
and forth.

Where

Quick Tip

You can use this sign to ask your
child to help find something. For
example, "Where is your coat?"
Your child may eventually combine
this sign with the sign for an object
he wants. An example of this would
be, "Where dog?"

Yes

Yes

"Nod" your "S" hand. See
Chapter 9 for how to sign the
letter "S."

Quick Tip

Teaching your child this sign will not
only give you the opportunity to say
"yes" but will help him communicate
his preferences as well!

You're Welcome

Move your flat hand in toward your body.

You're Welcome

Quick Tip

An automatic follow-up to "thank you"; be sure to sign it after your baby signs "thanks." It teaches another level of politeness and is also very cute!

Activity

Big and Little, Off and On

Here is an easy and fun way to teach both the concept and the signs for "big" and "little." Set up on a comfortable floor. Gather a variety of objects or toys around you. Help your child sort them into "big" or "little" piles (to avoid confusion, try to avoid "medium" things that might go either way).

After the items are sorted, practice "off" and "on" by placing one of his favorites on top of another toy, and then taking it back off again. You can also practice "please" and "thank you" in the same setting, as well as "want," "where," and "wait."

Activity

"If You're Happy and You Know It . . ."

An easy way to teach some of the emotion signs I have included here is to engage your toddler in a song, and "If You're Happy and You Know It" definitely fits the bill.

You can teach four signs with this song—"happy," "sad," "mad," and "sorry" (see illustrations below). Accompany each word with a matching facial expression and sign (signs in quotes).

If you're "happy" and you know it, show the sign (sign "happy" again)

If you're "happy" and you know it, show the sign (sign "happy" again)

If you're "happy" and you know it then your sign will surely show it

If you're "happy" and you know it, show the sign (sign "happy" again)

Happy, page 143

Sad, page 147

Mad, page 144

Sorry, page 147

Chapter

8

Teaching the Rainbow

Teaching Colors

Colors are something that you will want to wait to teach your child until she is older—approximately eighteen to twenty-four months. Of course, you can start earlier if your toddler shows interest!

The benefits of colors are many! They will come in handy at any time, even if your child has a few (or many) spoken words. They are really fun to learn, for one thing, and they can help your child differentiate between items. For example, if your daughter wants to wear her red dress, she can now let you know that is her preference.

To start teaching colors, I suggest starting with red, blue, or yellow. These primary colors are all distinct from one another and less likely to be confused. Start by pointing out the color whenever you see it. Once your child learns the sign don't be surprised if everything gets labeled with that color, even if it's purple or green! She will eventually sort it all out. Gently correct her by saying, "Wow, that's a beautiful 'green,' isn't it?"

After the primary colors are mastered, introduce purple, green, and orange. Follow that with black, white, and brown if you wish!

Using Felt Squares

One thing you can do to teach colors is to visit your local craft store and purchase squares of felt in a variety of colors. Be sure to select a medium blue as opposed to a lighter shade like baby blue to avoid confusion. Cut them into halves or quarters and keep them in a plastic pencil box (like children use at school). Lauren really enjoyed playing with her felt squares. We would spread out one of every color and she'd go through and sign every one. Since we had more than one of each color, we also would place down one set and give another set to her, one at a time, to play a matching game.

Black

Draw a line across your forehead, right above your eyebrows.

Black

Quick Tip

This reminds me of the eyebrows themselves and many people have dark ones—a good way to remember!

Blue

Shake your "B" hand. See Chapter 9 for how to sign the letter "B."

See Chapter 9 for how to sign the letter "B."

Blue

Quick Tip

The initial helps you remember this sign.

Brown

Run your "B" hand down the side of your face near your mouth. See Chapter 9 for how to sign the letter "B."

Quick Tip

The "B" helps you remember "brown" and the different placement helps remind you that it is not "blue."

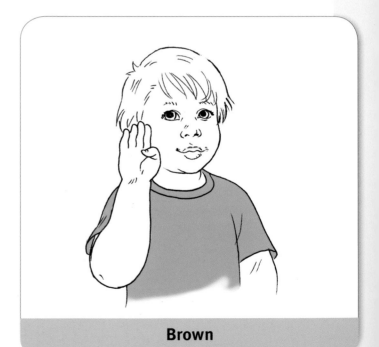

Brown

Colors

With your fingers pointing up, wiggle them in front of your mouth.

Quick Tip

This is a fun sign. Use it when you get out a box of crayons, for instance, or your baby's finger paints.

Colors

Green

Shake your "G" hand. See Chapter 9 for how to sign the letter "G."

Quick Tip

The initial "G" helps you remember that this is the sign for "green."

Green

Orange

Squeeze the air right in front of your chin.

Orange

Quick Tip

This is another fun sign. It reminds me of squeezing the juice out of an orange!

Purple

Shake your "P" hand.

Quick Tip

This sign's "P" will help you remember it. See Chapter 9 for how to sign the letter "P."

Purple

Red

Red

Brush your lip with your finger and then move it downward.

Quick Tip

This sign might remind you of red lips—that's how I am able to remember it.

White

Pretend you are grasping your shirt and pulling it away from your body.

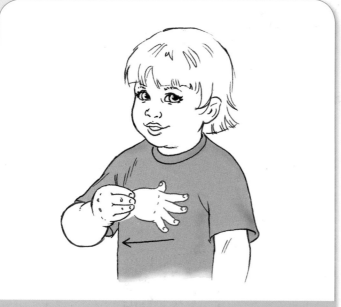

White

Quick Tip

Think of a white T-shirt when you sign this.

Yellow

Shake your "Y" hand. See Chapter 9 for how to sign the letter "Y."

Quick Tip

The "Y" will help you remember that this sign is for the color yellow.

Yellow

Chapter

9

Signing the Alphabet

Alphabet

• • •

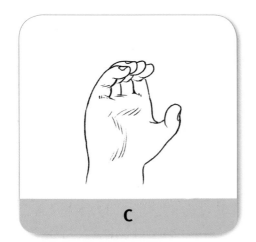

A

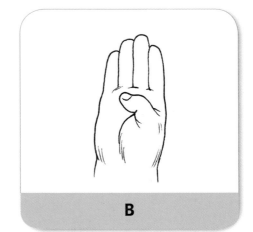

B

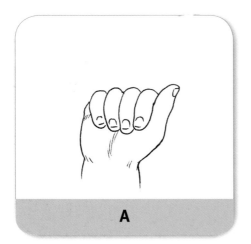

C

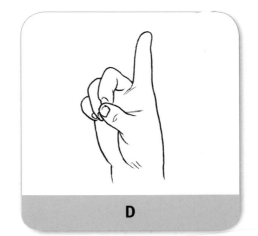

D

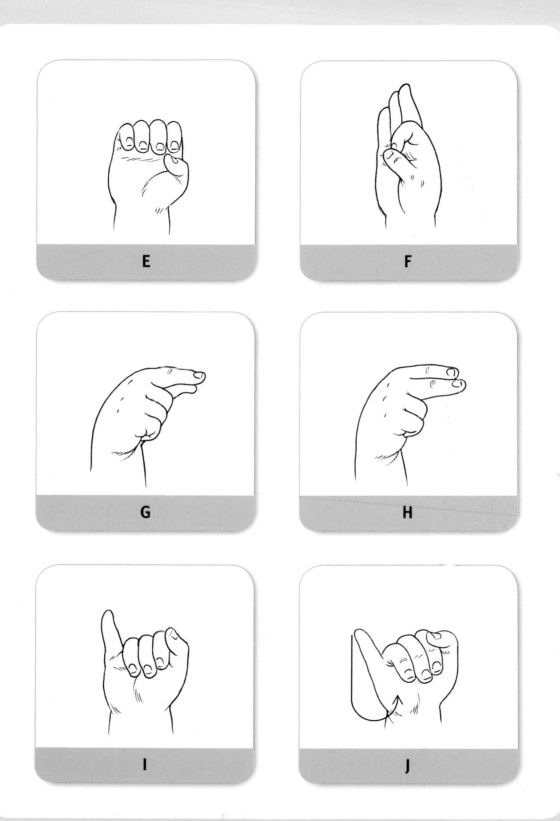

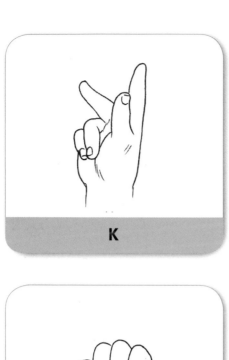

K

L

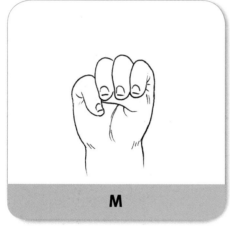

M

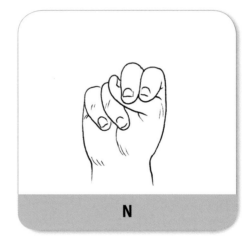

N

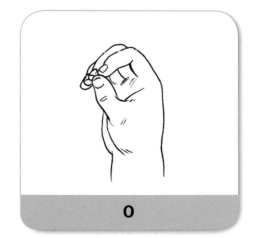

O

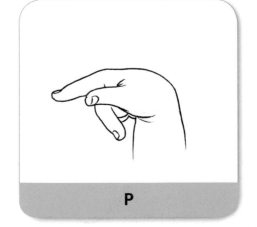

P

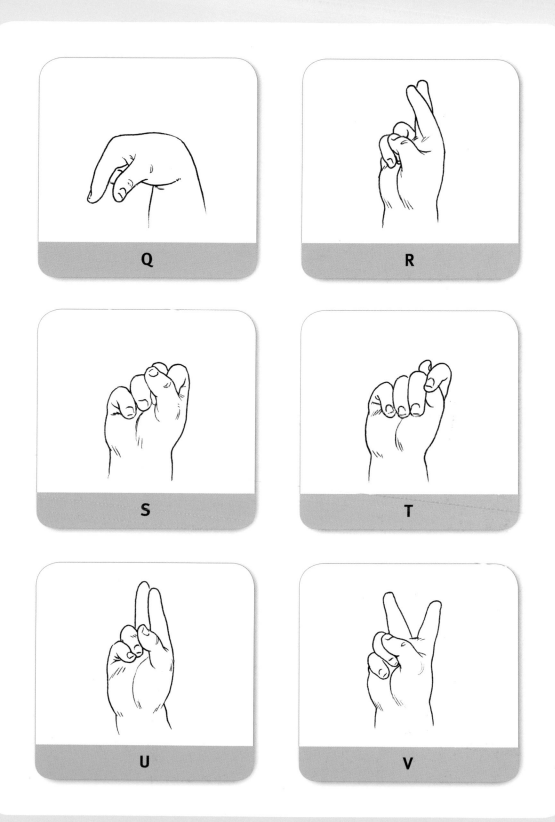

W

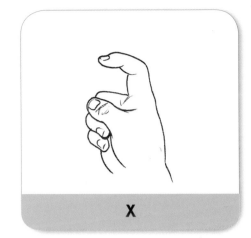

X

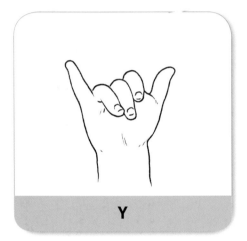

Y

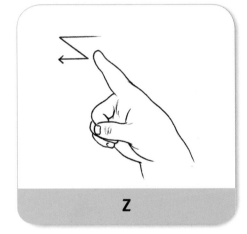

Z

Resources

• • •

On the Web

Author's Signing Site

www.signingbaby.com

Online ASL Dictionaries

http://commtechlab.msu.edu/sites/
   aslweb/browser.htm

www.aslpro.com

www.lifeprint.com

Various Baby Sign Language Programs/Companies

www.sign2me.com

www.babysigns.com

www.wideeyedlearning.com

www.mybabycantalk.com

www.babyseensign.com

www.signingtime.com

www.tinyfingers.com

www.weehands.com

Print Sign Language Dictionaries

Teach Your Tot to Sign: The Parents'
Guide to American Sign Language
Stacy A. Thompson
Gallaudet University Press, 2005

Acknowledgments

• • •

I would like to acknowledge first and foremost my family—my husband Kevin who is the most wonderful dad ever, and my trio of kids—Dagan, Corbin, and Lauren—who are the most beautiful creatures who have ever walked this planet. Add to the mix my parents and Nancy and John, who are the best grandparents I could have hoped for when I started having babies.

I would like to thank my wonderful friend Liz who helped get me this gig, as well as everyone else at Rockport Publishers who made my dreams of being an author that much more of a reality. Your guidance and expertise are top notch. Thank you to the beautiful children—Dylan, Eric, Eliana, and Jessica—who grace the pages of this book with their good looks.

I would also like to thank the following for their unending "virtual" support through this project and its accompanying nuttiness: Corrie, Erika, Robin, Hillary, Rachel, Joan, Amanda, Angela, and Jess. And don't forget Liz—the other Liz— McErin… thank you. Thanks also to "real life" best friends Sarah and Jessica— you know me better than I know myself so I wouldn't be complete without you.

And of course, I would like to thank all of the dedicated signing moms, dads, grandmas, grandpas, caregivers, aunts, and uncles. You are giving your child a wonderful tool that will benefit everyone for a long time to come. *Kudos to you!*

About the Author

• • •

Monica Beyer is the author of *Baby Talk* and has more than seven years of signing experience with her own family. She also runs her own website, www.signingbaby.com, where she helps other parents learn how to communicate with their children before they are able to talk. Monica graduated from Missouri Western State University with a BA in English, with an emphasis in Technical Communication. She lives with her husband Kevin and their three children—Dagan, Corbin, and Lauren—in St. Joseph, Missouri.

Sign Index

• • •